The Origin
Of Races And Color

Martin R. Delany

ISBN: 978-1-63923-172-0

Printed: March 2022

Cover Art By: Paul Amid

Published and Distributed By:
Lushena Books
607 Country Club Drive, Unit E
Bensenville, IL 60106
www.lushenabks.com

ISBN: 978-1-63923-172-0

PRINCIPIA OF ETHNOLOGY:

THE

ORIGIN OF RACES AND COLOR,

WITH AN

ARCHEOLOGICAL COMPENDIUM

OF

ETHIOPIAN AND EGYPTIAN CIVILIZATION,

FROM

YEARS OF CAREFUL EXAMINATION AND ENQUIRY,

BY

MARTIN R. DELANY,

*Formerly Physician, Surgeon and Practitioner in the Diseases of Women and Children;
Member of the International Statistical Congress, London, His Royal Highness Albert
Prince Consort of England, President; Member of the National Association for
the Promotion of Social Science, and Member of the Social Science Congress,
Glasgow, Scotland, 1860, Rt. Honorable Henry Lord Brougham and
Vaux, President; late Major in the United States Army, now one
of the Justices of Charleston, by Commission of the Governor.*

PHILADELPHIA:

HARPER & BROTHER, PUBLISHERS,

No. 413 WALNUT STREET.

1879.

DEDICATION.

To Right Honorable the Earl of Shaftesbury; Member of Her Brittanic Majesty's Privy Council; Knight of the Most Honorable Order of the Garter; Member of the Royal Society; Member and Patron of most of the British Institutions of Benevolence and Social Science, whether in England, Scotland or Ireland, this simple Treatise is most gratefully inscribed.

His Lordship will permit one whose obscurity and humble position in life, His Lordship is not expected to remember; but one who never can forget, that whether in the person of an escaping Hungarian Refugee, struggling Italian, obscure African Explorer of African descent, or Freedmen Jubilee Singers, in His Lordship all races have ever found one ready to stretch forth his hand, and reach down from his height and if possible, lift them up to his elevated position.

When a stranger and unknown, it was by the generosity of His Lordship, that the writer of this was forced to take a position among scientists in discussions of a learned council, for which no attainments that he possessed, could have induced him to claim a fitness, which at once gave him an unmerited place among the learned men of Europe.

Again, by the generosity of His. Lordship, and that of the great hearted nobleman, late Rt. Hon. Henry Lord Brougham and Vaux Ex-High Lord Chancellor, his humble name was favorably brought before the House of Lords, an honor that might be coveted by any man, however elevated.

DEDICATION.

It is for favors such as these, that his Lordship is begged to permit, a liberty which may be difficult to discern, whether it partakes most of presumption or impertinence. And the writer may dare venture to claim the moral aid of His Lordship, in this his second adventure, in the regeneration of his Race and Fatherland, and that Race the attainment of a promised inheritance.

He begs to remain His Lordship's most obliged, grateful, and very humble servant,

M. R. DELANY.

Charleston, S. C., May 6th, 1878.

CONTENTS.

PREFACE.

In presenting to the scientific and serious enquirer such a work as this, I may venture the opinion, that for the first time, public attention has been called to facts, essential to a satisfactory solution of the all-important question in social science, so befittingly put forth by the Duke of Argyll, in his ethnological enquiry, Primeval Man : " That question is not the rise of Kingdoms, but the Origin of Races * * * When and How did they begin ? * * * And in this feature of color it is remarkable that we have every possible variety of tint from the fairest to the blackest races, so that the one extreme passes into the other by small and insensible gradations." This then is the great mystery which this little treatise proposes to solve, as well as to show the first steps in the progress of Civilization, the origin and institution of Letters and Literature. On the delicate subject of the integrity of the Races, let it be also understood that we propose, so far as the Pure Races are concerned, to have once and forever settled that they are indestructible, as proven in this treatise. That, as in the substance and science of Chemistry, the two extremes, saccharine and acid—the most intense sweetness and the most intense sourness—are produced by the same material and essential properties, so is it in the substance and science of animal chemistry in the human family in relation to color or complexion of the skin. That the two extremes of color, from the most negative white—"including every possible variety of tint"—up to the blackest are all produced by the same material and essential properties of color. This much I have deemed it proper as a Preface to add, to prepare the mind of the reader for an enquiry which I may venture to say, he will not regret having made, and which may induce others of higher attainments to prosecute the subject to different conclusions. If in this I have been successful, in aiding to find the key to the discovery of the all-important subject of variety of complexions, or Origin of Races and Color, however little that aid, I shall have reached the zenith of my desire.

Charleston, May 6th, 1878.

CHAPTER I.

THE ORIGIN OF RACES AND COLOR.

This is a subject of very great interest to social science, which as yet has not been satisfactorily treated. We propose in this enquiry, to give our deductions and conclusions, after mature deliberation and much research.

The Singular and Plural theories of the Creation or Origin of Man, have been fully examined and duly considered, accepting the Mosaic or Bible Record, as our basis, without an allusion to the Development theory.

The theory of Champollion, Nott, Gliddon, and others, of the Three Creations of Man ; one Black, the second Yellow, and the last White, we discard, and shall not combat as a theory, only as it shall be refuted in the general deductions of this treatise. We have named these Three Races, in the order which they are said to have been created, the Black being first, consequently the oldest of the Human Family.

In treating on the Unity of Races as descended from one parentage, we shall make no apology for a liberal use of Creation as learned from the Bible. In this, we find abundant proof to sustain the position in favor of the Unity of the Human Race. Upon this subject ethnologists and able historians frequently seem to be at sea, without chart or compass, with disabled helm, floating on the bosom of chance, hoping to touch some point of safety ; but with trusty helm and well-set compass, we have no fears with regard to a direct and speedy arrival, into the haven.

CHAPTER II.

THE CREATION OF MAN.

Man, according to Biblical history, commenced his existence in the Creation of Adam. This narration is acceptable to us. The descendants of Adam must have been very numerous, as we read of peoples which we cannot comprehend as having had an existence, as "in the land of Nod, on the east of Eden, whither Cain went from the presence of the Lord and dwelt," where we are told his wife bore Enoch, his first born, though until this circumstance, had we known of the existence of but one woman, Eve the first and mother of Cain, who did not even have a daughter, so far as Moses has informed us in Genesis.

The history of Man from Adam to Noah is very short, as given by Moses in the first chapter in the Bible, and though we learn of the existence of communities and cities, as the first city Enoch, built by Cain in the land of Nod, called after his first born ; for aught we know, there were no legally established general regulations, but each head of a family ruled his own household according to traditional customs, his own desires or notions of propriety, or as circumstances or necessity required.

This view requires a division into periods of the historical events, from the Creation of Man, till after the confusion of tongues, and the dispersion of the people from the Tower of Babel. During the abode of Adam and Eve in the Garden of Paradise, we shall call the period of the "Original Law ;" from going out of the Garden till the dispersion from the Tower, the period of the "Law of Necessity ;" and after the dispersion on the Plains of Shinar, the period of "Municipal Law."

CHAPTER III.

THE ORIGINAL MAN.

Until the Dispersion, Races as such were unknown, but must have become recognized at that time, doubtless at the period of that event, which brings us to the enquiry, What was the Original Man?

There is no doubt that, until the entry into the Ark of the Family of Noah, the people were all of the One Race and Complexion; which leads us to the further enquiry, What was that Complexion?

It is, we believe, generally admitted among linguists, that the Hebrew word Adam (ahdam) signifies *red*—dark-red as some scholars have it. And it is, we believe, a well-settled admission, that the name of the Original Man, was taken from his complexion. On this hypothesis, we accept and believe that the original man was Adam, and his complexion to have been clay color or yellow, more resembling that of the lightest of the pure-blooded North American Indians. And that the peoples from Adam to Noah, including his wife and sons' wives, were all of one and the same color, there is to our mind no doubt.

There are those of the highest intelligence and deepest thoughts, in spite of their orthodox training and Christian predilections, who cannot but doubt the account of the Deluge, touching its universality. On this subject says the Duke of Argyll in his "Primeval Man:" "That the Deluge affected only a small portion of the globe which is *now habitable* is almost certain. But this is quite a different thing from supposing that the Flood affected only a small portion of the world which was *then inhabited.* The wide if not universal prevalence among the heathen nations, of a tradition preserving the memory of some such great catastrophe, has always been considered to indicate recollections carried by descent by the surviving few."

Believing as we do in the story of the Deluge, after the subsidence of the waters, there was but one family of eight persons who came forth from the Ark, to re-people the earth—Noah and his wife; their three sons and their wives. And according to Biblical chronology, from the birth of Cain, the first-born of Adam and Eve, to the subsiding of the waters of the Flood, the time was one thousand, six hundred and fifty-five years—1655—the Flood lasting but forty days and forty nights.

"And it came to pass, in the six hundredth and first year, in the first month, the first day of the month, the waters were dried up from off the earth: and Noah removing the covering of the Ark and looked, and behold, the face of the ground was dry." *Gen. C. viii, V. 13.* Now, what this six hundredth year means, we do not pretend to know; whether or not it alludes to the age of Noah, is inexplicable. For while chronology curiously enough would seem to make Noah only to have lived about one year after the Flood, the history tells us: "And Noah lived after the flood, three hundred and fifty years." *Gen. C. ix, V. 28.*

From the abatement of the waters to the building of the Tower, chronology makes it but one hundred and two years. This computation of time, would seem to agree very well with the number of people who must have accumulated as the offspring of the Four Families who came out of the Ark, the males of which were engaged on the Tower, at the time of the confusion of tongues, and dispersion abroad.

CHAPTER IV.

THE FAMILY OF NOAH.

Noah and family were Adamites, himself and wife being undoubtedly of the same color as that of their progenitors, Adam
and Eve.   And from the Garden of Eden to the Building of the
Tower, there certainly was but one race of people known as
such, or no classification of different peoples: "And the Lord
said, Behold, the people is one, and they have all one language;
and this they began to do: and now nothing will be restrained
from them which they have imagined to do." *Gen. C. xi, V. 6.*

Here we have inspired testimony of the unity of the people,
speaking one language, in consequence of which, they imagined
themselves all-powerful, setting all things at defiance.   Finally
to check this presumption, something had to be done, fully adequate to the end to be accomplished, which was the design of the
Divine will.   God has a purpose in all that he does, and his
purpose in the creation of man, was the promotion of his own
glory by the works of man here on earth, as the means of the
Creator.   And to this end man could best contribute, by
development and improvement in a higher civilization.

Could this be done by confining himself to a limited space
in one quarter of the earth, rearing up a building "whose top
may reach unto heaven"?   Certainly not; because as the people
were all one, and as "like begets like," the acquired manners,
habits, customs, and desires of these Tower builders, would have
been taught and schooled into their descendants, to the neglect
of all other employment and industries, confining themselves to
comparatively limited spaces, caring nothing for the require-

ments of community, desiring nothing but to "make brick and burn them thoroughly," and "build a city and a tower whose top may reach unto heaven," and "make for themselves a habitation and a name," lest they be "scattered abroad, upon the face of the whole earth." Here, just what God designed in the Creation of man, these descendants of Noah desired to prevent.

The Progress of Civilization, was God's requirement at the hands of man. How could this be brought about, seeing that the people were all one, "speaking one tongue," gathered together and settled in one place? Says his Grace, the Duke of Argyll: "The whole face of nature has been changed, not once, but frequently; not suddenly for the most part, perhaps not suddenly in any case, but slowly and gradually, and yet completely. When once this fact is clearly apprehended—whenever we become familiar with the idea that Creation has had a history, we are inevitably led to the conclusion that Creation has also had a method. And then the further question arises—What has this method been? It is perfectly natural that men who have any hopes of solving this question should take that supposition which seems the readiest; and the readiest supposition is, that the agency by which new species are created is the same agency by which new individuals are born."

How applicable is the above extract, to the subject under consideration. Civilization is promoted by three agencies, Revolution, Conquest, and Emigration; the last the most effective, because voluntary, and thereby the more select and choice of the promoters.

The first may come in two ways—morally and peacefully as the Coming of the Messiah; or physically and violently, as a civil war or conquest by military invasion, the worst agencies of civilization; but which do not fail to carry with them much that is useful into the country invaded. A moral revolution is always desirable as an agency in the promotion of civilization.

What then was the "method" of the Creator in effecting this desirable separation and scattering abroad of the people? Why simply the confusion of their tongues, by imparting to, or at least inspiring two divisions of them with a new tongue or dialect comprehended by all of those to whom it was imparted. Though on this subject the Bible is silent, it is reasonable to believe and safe to conclude, that one of the three divisions retained the old original Adamic tongue, so to speak, or that which they spoke when they commenced building ; and that one was that which followed after Shem, the progenitor of the Mongolian Race, and eldest of the sons.

By this "method" then, of an All-wise Creator, the people lost interest as communities in each other, and were thereby compelled to separate. And it will certainly be conceded by the intelligent enquirer, that there was a "method" in the manner, if allowed a paradox? But there were other changes said to be necessary to the final separation, in addition to that of the languages: the basis of race distinction, establishing the grand divisions. Is it to be supposed that God wrought a special miracle, by changing for the occasion the external physical characteristics of at least two divisions of the people? He did not. This was not His method ; He has a better and even wiser method than a miracle.

Again his lordship the Duke, in combating the Darwinian development theory—and for this we thank his Grace, as a most valuable endorsement of our humble position on the subject of the "Origin of Races and Color"—ere his lordship had written

his valuable " Primeval Man " : " It is not in itself inconsistent
with the Theistic argument, or with belief in the ultimate agency
and directing power of a Creative Mind.   This is clear since we
never think of any difficulty in reconciling that belief with our
knowledge of the ordinary laws of animal and vegetable production.   Those laws may be correctly, and can only be adequately
described in the language of religion and theology.   ' He who
is alone the Author and Creator of all things,' says the present
Bishop of Salisbury, ' does not by separate acts of creation give
being and life to those creatures which are to be brought forth,
but employs His living creatures thus to give effect to His will
and pleasure, and as His agents to be the means of communicating life.'   The same language," continues his Grace ; " might
be applied without the alteration of a word, to the origin of
species, if it were indeed true, that new kinds as well as new
individuals were created by being born."

CHAPTER V.

THE ORIGIN OF RACES.

We have shown the "method" of the Creator, in effecting
his design for man to " scatter abroad upon the face of the whole
earth ; " to " multiply and replenish it. "   But we have not yet
seen, how the division was brought about by the confusion of
tongues, so as to settle and harmonize the people, instead of dis-
tracting and discouraging them.   What mark of distinction could
there have been given to the multitudes of this "one people"

previous to separation, to enable them to recognize any individual of a separate division, without speaking? It must be seen, that such an act of All-wise interposition was essential, to enable each individual of any one of the now three grand divisions of the new tongues, when seen, to identify the other without speaking; otherwise, there would have been produced a "confusion worse confounded."

"And one of the questions on which testimony bears, is a question of paramount importance in determining the antiquity of the Human Family," says the Duke of Argyll. "That question is not the rise of kingdoms, but the origin of races. The varieties of man are a great mystery. The physical differences which these varieties involve may be indeed, and often are, much exaggerated. Yet these differences are distinct, and we are naturally impelled to ask When and How did they begin? The question When stands before the question How. The fundamental problem to be solved is this: can such a variety have descended from a single stock? And if they can, then must not a vast indefinite lapse of time have been occupied in the gradual development of divergent types?" This "mystery" we shall hope to solve by the aid of the light of science, and assistance of Divine authority, enabling us to discover the secrets of the laws of nature.

"And the Lord said, Behold the people is one, and they have all one language, let us go down and there confound their language." Behold the people are one; that is they are all of one stock, descended from the same parentage, all still living, consequently they consider themselves all one family. To separate this family, was the paramount object, and to sever their interests in each other, was necessary to this separation.

The sons of Noah were three in number: Shem, Ham and Japheth. That these three sons were the active heads of the people as directors and patriarchal leaders, there is no doubt.

There is to us another fact of as little doubt: that is, that these three sons of Noah all differed in complexion, and proportionate numbers of the people—their dependants in and about the city and around about the Tower—also differed as did the three sons in complexion. And these different complexions in the people, at that early period, when races were unknown, would have no more been noticed as a mark of distinction, than the variation in the color of the hair of those that are white, mark them among themselves as distinct peoples.

That Shem was of the same complexion as Noah his father, and mother—the Adamic complexion—there is no doubt in our mind. And that Ham the second son was swarthy in complexion, we have as little doubt. Indeed, we believe it is generally conceded by scholars, though disputed by some, that the word Ham means "dark," "swarthy," "sable." And it has always been conceded, and never as we know of seriously disputed, that Japheth was white.

Of one thing we are morally certain, that after the confusion of tongues, each one of these three sons of Noah, turned and went in different directions with their followers. These followers were just so many and no more, than those who spoke one and the same language. And there can be no reasonable doubt in our mind, that these people all were of the same complexion with each of the sons of Noah whom they followed. On leaving the Ark, they were one family, relatives, continuing together as "one people," all morally and socially blind and ignorant of any difference of characteristics personal, or interests general, as much so as a family of children with themselves toward the family, till years of maturity bring about a change. Hence, when the confusion took place, their eyes became open to their difference in complexion with each other as a division, preferring those of their kind with whom they went, thus permanently uniting their destiny.

Shem settled in Asia, peopling the country around and about the centre from where they scattered. Ham went to the south-west, and Japheth to the north-west. And it will not be disputed, that from then to the present day, the people in those regions where those three sons are said to have located— the three grand divisions of the Eastern Hemisphere: Asia, Africa and Europe—are, with the exceptions to be hereafter accounted for, of the distinct complexions of those attributed to Shem, Ham and Japheth ; Yellow*, Black and White. And this confusion of tongues, and scattering abroad in the earth, were the beginning and origin of races.

"But the great question," says the Duke of Argyll, "is not the rise of kingdoms, but the origin of races. When and How did they begin?" This we propose to show, in the next chapter, by an indisputable explanation of the origin of color by transmission of the parents.

* Yellow—called *brown* in South Carolina and the West Indies.

CHAPTER VI.

HOW COLOR ORIGINATES.

" Can such varieties, " enquires the Duke, "have descended from a single stock?" And why not? His Grace has truly said in another place quoted, "It is not in itself inconsistent with the Theistic argument, or with belief in the ultimate agency and directing power of a Creative mind. This is clear, since we never think of any difficulty in reconciling that belief with our knowledge of the ordinary laws of animal and vegetable reproduction."

Is it reasonable to suppose that there were necessarily original parents for all the varieties in every species of animals and vegetables? Must there have necessarily been a black and white cock, and a black and white hen, of all the varieties of fowls of every species? A black and white male and a black and white female of all the cattle stock of every variety of the same species? A black and white male, and a black and white female, of all animals canine and feline, of each variety of the same species? Were there necessarily separate creations for each of the same species of different colors among all these animals, beasts and fowls? Certainly not; and no hypothesis can make it affirmatively tenable. And just here, whence comes a black lamb, born of a white stock, a circumstance happening every year on almost every sheep farm, where every ram is white, and not the possibility of a black ram communicating with them?

This certainly is a theme, worthy of the attention of the leading minds in social science.

One remarkable fact of a law in procreation, which seems inexplicable, is the sexes always differ in color; the *male* invariably —with occasional exceptions—being *white,* and the *female, dark* or gray. We refer to the goose and gander. Why this should be so we know as little, and probably less, than we do why there should be races of man, differing in complexion, all from the same parent stock.

The Duke has wisely said, "Creation has had a method!" and again: "The same language might be applied, without the alteration of a word, to origin of species, if it were indeed true, that new kinds, as well as new individuals, were created by being born." Shem, Ham and Japheth, the three sons of Noah, we believe to have been and history so records them, as yellow, black, and white; and here hangs that mystery of the unity and brotherhood of man, that persons of three distinct complexions, could possibly be born of the same father and mother of one race and color. And that which seems to be enveloped in inexplicable concealment, is indeed to our mind, a comprehensible law of God's all-wise providence.

Let us take a peep into the laws of nature, and for a little, follow them as our guide. Our present familiarity with the spectroscope, gives us a knowledge of the properties of the sun, as transmitted through the rays, reflecting all the colors of the prism or rainbow. Solid matter of mineral subtances, we know to be among these properties.

Whatever has color then, whether animal, vegetable or mineral, receives these colors directly from the sun; that is, the essential properties that form or compose them. This is by a physiological process, called elaboration and selection, whether in animal, vegetable or mineral chemistry, or the natural functions of these systems, unaided by art. Of all the systems, general and particular, the human presents the most beautiful and comprehensive illustration of God's wonderful providence in the works of creation. But says his Grace of Argyll: "What of that vast continent of Africa? When and How did that negro race begin, which is both one of the most ancient and one of the most strongly marked among the varieties of man?" This is the cloud we design to dispel, and reveal the hidden secrets of a thousand ages.

The human body is covered by a structure composed of three distinct parts; the *cuticle* or external surface; the *rete mucosum*, middle or intermediate structure; and the *cutis vera* or true skin, underlying the other two, covering the whole surface of the fleshy parts or muscular system, called the hide in slaughtered animals.

The rete mucosum is a colorless jelly-like substance, composed of infinitesimal cells like a sponge or honey-comb. The cuticle or external surface is an extremely thin structure, colorless, and as perfectly clear and transparent as crystal glass. The upper surface of the cutis vera or true skin—that part in contact with the rete mucosum—is perfectly white. White is simply negative, having no color at all.

It will at once be observed, that the cuticle or external surface being transparent, the rete mucosum next below it being also colorless, and the surface of the cutis vera underlying all being white; that all human beings by nature are first white, at some period of existence, whether born white or not.

The cells of the rete mucosum are filled with limpid fluid, and whatever the complexion of an individual or race, the coloring matter is deposited in the cells of the rete mucosum, mixed with the limpid fluid. This is deposited there by the process of elaboration and selection in animal chemistry, a function simply of physiology.

This coloring matter in the Caucasian or white race is *rouge* as we shall term it, the essential properties which give redness to the rose. When a white person blushes, red matter rushes into the cells of the rete mucosum, then recedes, leaving them as before, colorless, and the complexion white. When a white person has rosy cheeks or "ruby lips," there is a fixed deposit of rouge in those parts; but where they are pale and "colorless," there is an absence of rouge or coloring matter in the rete mucosum. In the Mongolian or yellow race of Asia, the coloring matter is the same—rouge—modified by peculiar elaboration, and uniformly infused into the rete mucosum, giving the yellow tinge —one of the known properties of the sun's rays—to the complexion.

And in the African or black race of Africa, the coloring matter *is the same* as that in the other two races, being *rouge* concentrated, which makes a pigment—the *pigmentum nigrum* of physiology—or a black matter. Thus the color of the blackest African is produced by *identically the same* essential coloring matter that gives the "rosy cheeks and ruby lips," to the fairest and most delicately beautiful white lady.

For illustration, to prove that concentrated rouge or concrete redness is black, take blood caught in a vessel, let it cool and dry up by evaporation of the liquid part; when condensed in a solid mass, it becomes perfectly black, more so than the blackest human being ever seen. Look again at the fruits: black berries, black cherries, poke berries and the like. From greenness, discoloration goes on till approaching a whiteness, when a faint redness ensues, gradually increasing to a deep red, which merges into blackness, the intense color of red.

Take now this clot of dried blood, and these fruits, macerate them in water and you have not a black, but assuredly a red solution. Compare these deep red fruits called black with the color of the blackest person in complexion, and there will be the most remarkable contrast between the fruit and the skin.

May it not by this be seen, in the language of the Duke, that "new kinds as well as new individuals can be born?" Cannot God's wonderful and inscrutable providence be seen in this simple but comprehensibly beautiful law of procreation? It certainly can.

Here we see that the first son of Noah, Shem, was born with a high degree of a certain complexion or color; the second son, Ham, with a higher degree, or intensity of the same color, making a different complexion; and the third son, Japheth, with the least of the same color, which gives an entirely different complexion to either. The three brothers were all of the *same color— rouge*—which being possessed in different degrees simply, gave them different complexions.

Was there any miracle in this; any departure from the regular order of the laws of nature, necessary to the production of these three sons of a different complexion by the same mother and father of one complexion? Certainly not; as it is common to see parents of one complexion, and hair and eyes of one color, produce children with hair and eyes of various colors. Then the same laws in physiology, which produced the former of these variations, also produced the other; but for His all-wise purposes— doubtless the production of fixed races of man—the effect was placed upon the *skin* instead of the eyes and hair.

For the convenience of classification, these complexions may be termed *positive, medium*, and *negative*. Ham was positive, Shem medium, and Japheth negative. And here it may be remarked as a curious fact, that in the order of these degrees of complexion which indicated the ardor and temperament of races they represented, so was the progress of civilization propagated and carried forward by them. But is it still in doubt, that the color of the African is homogeneous with that of the Mongolian and Caucasian Races, or that either is identified with that of the other? In this, too, we summon the incontestable laws of nature. In this we have reference simply to the three original races: Mongolian, African and Caucasian, or Yellow, Black and White.

Physiology classifies the admixture of the races by a cross between the White and Black, as a Mulatto; between the Mulatto and White, a Quadroon; between the Quadroon and White, a Quintroon; between the Quintroon and White, a Sextaroon; between the Sextaroon and White, a Septaroon; between the Septaroon and White, an Octoroon. The same numerical classifications are given a like number of crosses between the offsprings of the Black and Mulatto, with a prefix of the adjective black; as a Black Quadroon, and so on to Octoroon. A cross between the American Indian and a White, is called a Mustee or Mustezo; and a cross between the Indian and Black, is called a Sambo or Zambo; and the complexional distinction is precisely the same, either white or black, as that of the offspring between the Mulatto and a White or Black. Here the beauty and wisdom of that Divine law, creating man with a medium complexion, from whence all others originated, is apparent, the Indian being of the Adamic or original complexion.

Now, what is here to be observed as an exact and, with little variation, almost never failing result, in this law of procreation between the African and Caucasian, or White and Black races is, that these crosses go on with a nicety of reducing and blending the complexion, till it attains its original standard to either pure white or pure black, on the side by which the cross is continued from the first.   By this it is seen that each race is equally *reproducing, absorbing,* and *enduring,* neither of which can be extinguished or destroyed, all admixtures running out into either of the original races, upon the side which preponderates.

This is an important truth, worthy the attention and serious consideration of the social scientist, philosopher, and statesman. That two races as distinct as the Black and White, may dwell together in their purity, is marvellously true, because whatever of crosses may take place, they will run out into purity on one side or the other, by intermarriage on either side continued.* And how wonderfully typical of the first or original man, is this crossing of the races; the offspring of the white and black being yellow, precisely the complexion of Adam, the First Man !

Shem, Ham and Japheth, the sons of Noah and wife, who were Adamites and of one complexion, were themselves of three different complexions, as a means in the providence of God's economy, to the accomplishment of his ends in the progress of civilization.

---

* Hon. Henry Clay, the great statesman, years ago when the humanitarian discussions concerning the two races in America were attracting public attention, in an able letter, suggested a prohibition to the importation of the black race, and a continual cross, when they would become extinct.   The distinguished statesman had by observation, evidently become acquainted with the fact, that the black race could be absorbed by the white, without probably understanding at all that this was a mutual and unalterable law of procreation between the two races, applying equally to both white and black.

"And the Lord said, Behold the people is one." They were one in descent, one in family, one in interest, one in design, and one in purpose ; having one language, they had no other thought than remaining together. And so doubtless would have continued as one, had not some sufficient cause transpired, to completely break up their interests, and compel them to a forced separation. "So the Lord scattered them abroad from thence, upon the face of all the earth " ; and this separation of these three brothers was the *Origin of Races.* Each of these brothers headed and led his people with a language, and in all reasonable probability a complexion similar to his own, each settling the then known three parts of the earth : Asia, Africa and Europe.

And God's design in the creation of the races was accomplished, because it fixed in the people a desire to be separated by reason of race affinity. To "replenish and multiply," or the peopling of the earth, was a principal command by God, given to man ; and by this was carried out one of the intentions of the Divine will in creation.

Can his Grace, the Duke of Argyll, now see "when and how did that negro race begin ?"

CHAPTER VII.

SPECIAL EXPLANATION ON COLOR.

"What causes the color of the negro'; what is it, and of what does it consist?" has been an enquiry of the deepest interest through all ages, among all nations, with such varied speculations, that we have concluded, in addition to the foregoing chapter, to make a special explanation on color.

Said Herodotus the learned Greek, and "father of history": "The Egyptians and Ethiopians have black skins and woolly hair." Also said Strabo; "The Ethiopians are black and woolly haired;" his allusion and astonishment evidently being more at the color of their skin, than the texture of the hair. And exclaiming with wonder, said Pliny: "For who has believed the account about the Ethiopians before he saw them?"

In this special explanation, we shall feel more at liberty to summon physiology to our aid, than to intrude into other pages the full text of these.

The human *skin* as before explained, consists of three structures; the cuticle or epidermis at the surface; the rete mucosum immediately next and below; the cutis vera, corsium, dermis, or true skin, lying at the base of all. The first is a thin transparent colorless structure, like the thin layers of a bladder, or tissue seen between the leaf-fat of fine mutton.

This is simply that which is rubbed off by abrasion from the back of the hand or leg, leaving no other wound than a fresh tender looking place, when it is said one skinned his hand or leg, by abrasion or rubbing against something. The second is a jelly like colorless substance or structure, and that which begins to throw out on the surface, where the skin is rubbed off, little glob-ules, or clear drops of a liquid substance. The third is the true skin or hide which the butcher takes off slaughtered animals, and is tanned as leather. The upper surface of the true skin next to the rete mucosum or middle structure, is also colorless or white naturally, like the tissue of leaf-fat.

The rete mucosum or middle structure of the skin, now be-comes the most important subject of investigation, the "opening of the second seal" of the great mystery of the revelation of col-or, answering the question, "When and How did that negro race begin?" In this again, rete mucosum, the coloring matter which gives complexion to all races in general and every individ-ual in particular, lies. It is cellular, sponge or honey-comb like, each cell being a vesicle or little pouch, capable like a blad-der of holding whatever in a liquid state, enters it.

In the white race these cells or pouches are mainly empty or partially filled with a colorless transparent substance, clear like water. But whenever color—as a flush in the face from blushing, anger or any other emotion—is seen, it is caused by the presence of *red* matter at the moment rushing into these little cells of the rete mucosum. When paleness ensues it is caused by the color-ing or red matter leaving and remaining out of them during the paleness.

For a better comprehension without regard to chemical prop-erties, all red matter will be termed *rouge,* our object being not to discuss the elementary principles of matter, but show on this im-portant enquiry of color, cause and effect.

Elaboration and selection, as in the preceding chapter stat-ed, is a first process in the physiology and functional chemistry of all things, animate and inanimate—animal, vegetable, and min-

eral.   And whether in the blood-root, beet, cam-wood, poke-ber-
ry, currant, cherry, black-berry, dahlia, rose, all flowers and
fruits as vegetable; the gills of a gobbler, comb and gills of a
cock, red-headed reptiles, red plumaged heads and cape feathers
of birds and other fowls as animals; and the precious stone ruby,
as mineral, all contain the same essential coloring matter, rouge, by
the same process of elaboration and selection.

What is the coloring matter which enters the cells of the rete
mucosum of the African race producing the "jet black" complexion, as it is termed?   Is it homogeneous or heterogeneous
—of the same or a different nature, to that which composes the
color or complexion of the other races?   This is the all important enquiry, to answer which satisfactorily, puts at rest forever,
the enquiry of ages, and opens the book of mysteries on this subject.   If homogeneous, the black race has a common origin with
the other two—Mongolian and Caucasian—races; but if heterogeneous, none with Noah's, and consequently, none with Adam's
race.

All coloring matter which enters into the human system may
be termed pigment,—*pigmentum*—as before intimated; that in
the fair race being *red*, that in the tawny being yellow in appearance, the red being modified by elaboration according to the
economy of the system of each particular race.   In the Caucasian,
it is in its most simple elementary constituent; in the Mongolian,
in a more compound form.   But that which gives complexion to
the blackest African, is the *same red* matter; *concentrated rouge*,
in its most intensified state.

Why should an elaboration and selection of the same coloring matter take place so differently in the black race from that of
the other two races?   Or why should an elaboration and selection

of the same coloring matter take place so differently in the yellow race from that of the white, or be different in either, if in reality descended from the same common origin—one parent stock? Simply because it is in accordance with the economy of the Creator, to give a general and unerring reproductive system, to each race whereby it should always be known, by its own peculiar characteristics; as also it was a part of His economy to give each individual of the same race, a particular reproductive system of temperament, whereby the same parents as father and mother, produce children of different temperaments and different color of eyes and hair as before mentioned, as may be seen in almost every family of the white race.

It is needless to pursue this part of the enquiry further, as just here is where the mysterious, inscrutable wisdom of God comes in. And here also may most impressively be applied, that beautiful philosophical conclusion of the Duke of Argyll in " Prim'eval Man, " " that creation has also had a method. " Can not we see something of this " method " here?

This is morally, physically, and consequently scientifically, in perfect harmony with the variations and departure or changes from the most simple elementary color of the one, to the extremely intensified color of the other of the aboriginal progenitors of the three fixed races. Should, from its blackness, the essential properties of the coloring matter of the African or negro race be disputed, let further enquiry answer. Take any or all such fruits known as *black*, previously referred to in these pages; first green, then whitish or colorless, next a slight red, deepening daily, to the final intense red or blackness in color. Has the fruit during these changes simply increased the property of color by adding particles of coloring matter, or has it lost its original properties of red by attaining the hue of blackness? It has simply increased in color matter of the same nature, till it attained the highest degree of that color which, intensified, is simply black, that is all. Prove it, as illustrated by the maceration of a black blood-clot in water, and you will have the proof at hand.

Why is it that an increase in redness attains a hue of blackness? Simply because, as in the case of the black blood-clot referred to, the particles are compressed into a solid mass, the intenseness of which is black in hue; but when macerated in water, the particles become separated, when they reflect their true color, red.

The color, then, of the negro, over which for ages there has been so much speculation in every conceivable thought almost, is no more nor less than *concentrated rouge;* the same color which in giving blackness of complexion to his skin, gives also in turn, the most delicate rosy tint to the ruddy cheeks and ruby lips of the lily white skin of the proudest and most beautiful white lady of the Caucasian race.

This fact is still more apparent, when observing that color in the deepest dye, as it lessens in intensity upon the lips of some black persons, gradually terminating in a most striking *scarlet-red* on the inner part of the lip at the verge of the teeth, impressively reminding us of the Song of Solomon in memory of his black beauty, the Queen of Sheba: "Thy lips are a thread of scarlet." *Song Sol., C. iv, V. 3.*

One illustration more, by comparison. Take any of the blackest berries, as currants, whortle-berries, poke-berries, mulberries, black-berries, as called, or black-heart cherries, and on close inspection with the eye, the hue will be really a deep or dark purple. Then let the hand of the blackest person be placed on a dish or other vessel filled with this fruit, or the fruit be placed in juxtaposition with the skin of such person, and it will be found to be a dark red compared with the fruit, really a purple. So that the *color* of the negro race, the African, is really a *purple* and nothing else.

But purple involves a mixture of red and blue, and implies the presence of *blue* in the blood, as all color elaborated in the system comes through the blood, as the only medium of circulation and deposit through the system.

Certainly it is true, or whence come the "blue veins" of the white race shown through the colorless rete mucosum and transparent epidermis; and whence the blue eyes so much prided in by that race, as one of the characteristics of race superiority as claimed? Also the blue, developed in certain pathological conditions of the system, on the skin of persons of both sexes of the white race? Blue, then, is a constituent element of the blood, or it could not be developed in any condition of the system, normal or abnormal. Hence, then, this purple color of the negro; a color that has long been derisively applied to the natives of Africa and the West Indies by foreign sailors and seamen of the white race; by the epithet "blue skins," as the American sailors styled the Haitians; and "purple skins," as applied to the natives of Africa by British seamen, as the writer himself once heard when a passenger on a British steamer some years ago, on the coast of Africa.

And as significantly bearing upon this important subject, it may not be out of place here to note the fact, that purple, as a dress color was originated in Africa; the Ethiopians and Egyptians who had the most delicate observation of color, adopted it as a royal choice, and must have had a significance as all of their designs had, which was most probably, emblematic of the color or complexion of their kings and queens, and therefore, the royal families. Yellow is also a constituent of the blood, as seen in the eyes, the bile, jaundice, yellow fever, and other pathological conditions of the system, which takes its place, in the modification of complexion in the human race.

It is known by medical men, that *arterial* blood never coagulates or clots, and is known as the red or scarlet blood ; that *venous* blood coagulates or clots, and is known as the blue blood. Can not the wisdom of Providence be seen without the supposed intervention of a miracle, in creating the color of the negro by a "method," in the process of elaboration and selection, a regular established law of physiology, by an adequate quantity of the red and blue bloods blending, to form the deep purple for the negro complexion? More on this point is needless ; the law by which it may be done is complete and comprehensive, and almost defies controversy.

How strikingly is this fact of a variety of complexion arising from the same essential properties of color and stock, beautifully carried out and illustrated in what we are taught scientifically to look upon as one of the lowest orders of animated nature, the mollusca, which on certain bright, calm, sunny days, may be seen floating on the surface of the ocean, facetiously termed by seafaring men, "Portuguese men of war," whose tissue-like sheets spread to the breeze, vary in every hue, from a clear, bladder, bubble-like whiteness, increasing in the faintest rose-colored tint, to the deepest purple, till it reaches the most intense dahlia-like blackness. All these colors may sometimes be seen at one and the same time, looking like a flower garden; no doubt the immediate offspring of the same individual family. It is singular, that the lowest and highest orders of animal life— the mollusca and man—should exhibit as they do, so truthfully, distinctly and clearly, this great mystery of the Divine economy, in giving variety of complexion.

And what of the *Albino,* the *clearest* and *whitest* of which are born of pure black, African or negro parents? Could not a *pure white* and a *pure black* child have as easily been produced from parents of a precisely *medium color* as this extreme, especially when designed to subserve the ends of perfecting the establishment of races in the economy of the Creator? Certainly they could, and we think this point undisputed. Concede this, and nothing more, and we shall have incontrovertibly established the *unity* of races and *color* of the whole human family.

That like the vegetable kingdom, every seed, from that of a grain of mustard to a cocoanut, there is but one uniform plan and structure for reproduction; the substance of the seed which is the kernel, consisting of nothing more than the impacked leaves of whatever tree or plant produced it; and as in the animal kingdom, in the anatomical structure of all vertebrates, from fish to man, the Divine Creator had but *one plan;* so in the human races, running through all the *various shades of complexion,* there is but *one color,* modified and intensified from negative to the extremest positive, as seen from the purest white, in *all intermediate colors,* to the purest black. This is the solution of the problem which reveals to us the great mystery of the races of man.

This truth as proven in regard to color, is but another evidence to show in the language of that great master in natural science, Agassiz: "That the animal kingdom especially has been

constructed upon a plan which pre-supposes the existence of an
intelligent being as its Author. " And we may be permitted to
add: there is no part of this great subject—the creation of man
—more convincing of the existence and wisdom of God as our
Creator, than the subject now under consideration. Like the
flowers of the fields, it is that which presents itself to the view of
every one, making its own impression, and causing seriously enquiring reflections, as to the cause of the " variety of colors. "

We have confined our explanations to the description of the
three original races, as we hold and believe that the Malay* is
simply the product of these three great races by admixture, and
therefore, an off-shoot or composite race, and not an original
one. We also believe that the North American Indian is an offspring of the Mongolian or original yellow race of Asia, a descend-
ant of Shem.

From what has been herein adduced, may not his Grace the
Duke be now more reconciled, in his able enquiry wherein he
says: "strongly marked as the varieties of man now are, the variation is strongest in respect to color, which in all organisms is
notoriously the most liable to modification and to change. And
in this feature of color it is remarkable that we have every possible
variety of tint from the fairest to the blackest races, so that the
one extreme passes into the other by small and insensible gradations. "

*Malay, an abnormal race.

CHAPTER VIII.

THE PROGRESS OF RACES.

When by Divine command to go forth through the earth, the separation took place, the people led by the three sons of Noah, began a new progress in life, as three distinct peoples, of entirely different interests, aims and ends. Shem remained in Asia; Ham went to Africa, and Japheth journeyed to Europe, permanently and forever severing their connexion with each other, henceforth becoming different peoples and divided as though they never had been united. And then the different Races of the Human Family had just begun. At this time, also, we reckon the commencement of the period of municipal law.

Previous to this time, doubtless headed and directed by Patriarchs or fathers of families, they had little else than traditional precepts to govern them, and neither books nor literary records of any kind. Their laws, then, must have been few and simple, private and public, restricted and limited, there being no large cities or towns requiring many police regulations.

Of the three sons, the history of the second, Ham, in the earliest is fraught with more interest than that of either of the others. Four sons he had : Cush, Mizraim, Phut and Canaan. All of these, from all that we are able to learn, except Canaan, accompanied him to Africa, settling in different parts, where they may be readily traced : Canaan settling in Asia closely on the borders of Africa; his father, Ham himself, permanently locating in Egypt, where doubtless he was deified as the Jupiter Ammon of Africa. Cush, the eldest son, pushed farther into the country, founding the Kingdom of Ethiopia, with Meroe as the capital. Cush was the father of Nimrod, a mighty Prince, who did not follow the fortunes of his father and three of his brothers, but remained in Asia, becoming the first ruler after the Dispersion, a great Monarch, carrying conquest, and building great cities, establishing an extensive and powerful government. Of him the Scriptures say: "He began to be a mighty one in the earth, a mighty hunter before the Lord."

The progress of civilization now seems fairly to have begun by the establishment of extensive municipal governments. Chaldea and Assyria were included in this mighty Empire, which appears to have been almost unlimited in extent of territory.

The African branch of this family is that which was the earliest developed, taking the first strides in the progress of the highest civilization known to the world, and for this cause, if for no other, it may be regarded as the oldest race of man, having doubtless centuries prior to the others, reared imperishable monuments of their superior attainments.

It has been thought by some able writers that the different complexions of the three brothers, had been caused by the confusion of tongues. This does not follow, as we have shown in another place that the complexions doubtless all existed previous to that event, to which the attention of the people became particularly attracted, as they had now become divided.

Noah, we are told in the Bible, was six hundred years old previous to the flood, and none but himself and wife, his three sons, and their wives—eight persons in all—entered the ark; all other people, whatever their complexion, having been destroyed by the flood. It is singularly remarkable, that of the

three sons, though all married, none had children.   How wonderful, though naturally simple, is this part of the plan of the
Divine arrangement.   Noah lived three hundred and fifty years
after the flood, when he died ; and his sons are all known to
have survived him.   One of the commands given by God to
these four extraordinary families was : "Be fruitful and multiply,
and replenish the earth."

We recall here a fact in proof of the nearness or unity of the
human family, which is singularly applicable; it is, that one
cross from the middle or medium complexion—yellow—either
way, white or black, produces the quadroon nearly white or black.
Indeed, the white quadroon or black quadroon, is simply either
a white or black person, and should be classed as such, which
is done by the black race, and also by the white in all countries
except in the Western Hemisphere, especially the United States
where the blacks have been held in bondage, and thereby degraded.

At the entering into the ark, two of the sons of Noah—
Ham and Japheth—alone differed in complexion from all the
other people then on all the face of the earth ; one black, the
other white ; as Noah and wife, and Shem and wife, as well as
the two wives of Ham and Japheth, must have been of the original complexion, yellow or "red," the standard Adamic color.
The three sons, previous to entering the ark, had no children, or
took none with them, if the Bible be not at fault in the history
of this family.   This important fact proves that up to this
period there was no mixed race, nor mixture of colors among
the people previous to the exodus from the ark.

Three hundred and fifty years—the length of time that
Noah lived after the flood—would produce an immense popula-

tion under the command of God to "be fruitful, and multiply, and replenish the earth." And since there were two yellow men and women, as men and wives, Noah and Shem with their wives to one black and white man—Ham and Japheth, with their wives who were yellow, of the medium complexion, then the increase of progeny might have gone on at the ratio of two yellows to one black and one white—black quadroon and white quadroon —which, no doubt, to our mind may account for the Mongolian or yellow race to this day outnumbering in population by probably two to one, either black or white, the African or European race.

The Three Races it would seem, went steadily along on the increase, each holding its ratio with the other, the one which occupied the most favorable position in point of geographical location, advancing the most rapidly in the progress of civilization. This subject of the Origin of Races, is of vast importance and unabating interest. How beautifully comprehensive then is this plan, this "method" of the Divine economy— natural, simple, and almost indisputable!

Nimrod, the son of Cush—"Kush," in Ethiopian—commenced as previously mentioned, his grand intellectual, moral— moral because pleasing in the sight of the Lord, before whom he "began to be a mighty hunter"—physical, and topographically structural improvements, which left their impress on two of the mightiest empires known to antiquity—Assyrian and Babylonian.

CHAPTER IX.

PROGRESS OF THE BLACK RACE.

" The Sons of Ham ; Cush, Mizraim, Phut and Canaan, and the sons of Cush ; Seba, and Havilah, and Sabtah, and Raamah, and Sabtecha, and Cush begat Nimrod." The sons of Cush as here seen were six in number, and if born in the order here given, the youngest, Nimrod, was he who first arose to that eminence of national greatness as a Monarch, which till this day has made his name famous among the greatest princes.

From all that can be gathered by research, Cush took up'his line of march—his father Ham among his followers—south-westerly, settling a colony in Asia, contiguous to Egypt, on the territory terminating at the Isthmus of Suez, known as "the land of Midian." How long he remained here, cannot be ascertained, but he with his father Ham, is known to have entered through the Isthmus into Africa, Ham settling permanently on the Delta, or territory formed by the mouths of the river Nile ; while Cush pushed inwardly up the Nile, farther into Africa. From what we are able to glean from history, it is very probable that his next brother, Mizraim, Ham's second son, was left at the head of the people, as Prince of Midian, when Cush and Ham left ; Mizraim in time either being sent for by his father, or from the growing importance of the little kingdom, left Midian under his next brother Phut, the third son of Ham, as Prince of Midian, when he joined his father Ham in Egypt, as co-ruler of the people.

That the rule of Cush extended from the Nilotic borders of Egypt quite in toward the interior of the country, the whole of which was called Ethiopia, is indisputable ; and it is a fact which learned men will not dispute, that in the early settlement of those countries, Egypt and Ethiopia were united Kingdoms, under the joint rule of three Princes, father and two sons. Says a great work published in London in 1705: "Pliny relates, that Ethiopia was anciently divided into forty-five kingdoms." Again says the same author: "According to Diodorus Siculus, the laws of Ethiopia agreed in substance with those of Egypt." Again: "Jupiter Ammon according to the Greek and Latin authors, seems to have been the principal object of religious worship in Ethiopia;" and in a foot note he continues: "Diodorus Siculus tells us, that the Ethiopians valued themselves upon their being the first nation that had a religious establishment. They believed that for this reason," adds he, "their sacrifices were more acceptable to the gods than those offered by any other people, which notion," continues Diodorus, "Homer himself seems to countenance, when he introduces Jupiter attended by the other gods, as present at an anniversary sacrifice, or grand entertainment prepared for him by the Ethiopians."

We have, we think, sufficiently shown the proximity of Ethiopia and Egypt in customs, to justify the belief in their once unity of national interests. Ham, the head, first prince and ruler in Egypt, in the course of time dies of old age, leaving the rule to Mizraim, when the old King, Ham, is at once deified and worshipped as a god, under the name of *Jupiter Ammon*, and symbolic representation of a ram, having the head of a ram upon the body of a man; or the head of a man with the great horns of a ram, as he was represented both ways. He is also consecrated with the royal dynastic title of Rameses I.

Mizraim in turn when passing away, was also worshipped as a god, symbolized as an oxen—a bull—taking the royal title of

Rameses II.   The reign of this prince in succession to his father is said to have been magnificent in the extreme, and conjointly with his brother Cush, a matchless prince in the adjoining kingdom, Ethiopia, it is believed was commenced as an international policy, these invaluable intellectual blessings to the human race, of propagating the science of letters.   That hieroglyphics were, till this period, the only method of communicating by written signs, there is no doubt.   These two great princes acted in concert for the mutual benefit of both countries, in the erection of the Pyramids—a style of architectural monuments with which they were familiar, having themselves taken part in the construction of the Tower of Babel—the Catacombs, the enlargement and architectural improvement of their common countries and principal cities, as Meroe in Ethiopia, and Thebes in Egypt, pushed forward with an energy and determination unsurpassed, if equalled, in the history of man.

The three principal Pyramids, no doubt, were originally erected for and dedicated to these three great princes, father and two sons; Jupiter Ammon or Rameses I. Sesostris or Rameses II.; and when he also in time had been "gathered to his fathers," Cush was deified and worshipped under the symbol of a dog, with the divine complimentary title of Osiris, because he was the great leader of the family to Africa; he was also consecrated with the royal dynastic title of Rameses III. and this is thought to have been the time when Ethiopia and Egypt were united under the rule of one prince.   It was doubtless his kingdom which extended from the Nile to the Niger, and thus gave rise to the idea of calling the two rivers one, or the Niger the wife of the Nile, representing them as the great serpent guarding the Garden of the Hesperides.

" According to Diodorus Siculus, the laws of Ethiopia agree in substance with those of Egypt. This," continues the same author, " the Ethiopians accounted for by asserting that Egypt was first peopled by a colony drawn from their country. In order to evince this point, they mention the land of Egypt to have been at first, for a considerable period, entirely covered with water, and afterwards raised gradually, so as to become inhabited by fresh accessions of mud the Nile brought every year out of Ethiopia. This is likewise confirmed by Herodotus, who affirms Egypt to be the gift of the Nile, and that the whole region, except the territory of Thebes, in the time of Meus was one continued morass." Thus says the great historian, from whom we have frequently quoted, and this goes far toward es· tablishing the belief of the first colonial settlement in Africa being on the upper regions of the Nile by Cush with his father Ham, in consequence of the daily inundation of the Delta of Lower Egypt by the tide, until the alluvial deposits from the waters of the river, elevated that low flat land, encouraging the people from Ethiopia or Upper Egypt, to go down to cultivate rice, which required embankments, making the territory habitable like that of Holland, by dikes, when the old head, Ham, surrounded by his colony, commenced the establishment of his government. And the culture of rice as a bread stuff of that newly settled region, would have been a great incentive to the rapid growth and fame of that country, on account of which may have been the main cause of Mizraim leaving Midian, if not, indeed, being sent for by the old Prince, his father, who found the demands of a rapidly growing nation too great for the capacity of his fast declining energy.

"As the Ethiopians agreed with the Egyptians in most of their laws, their splendid funerals, the deification of their princes, the several colleges of priests, circumcision, and, in fine, most of their sacred and civil institutions, it is highly probable that the same arts, science and learning, as well as religion prevailed among both nations.   Nay, this seems to be expressly asserted by Diodorus Siculus, when he informs us, that not only the same kind of statutes, but likewise the same hieroglyphic figures and characters were used in Egypt and Ethiopia, since it is generally allowed that those were the repositories of Egyptian wisdom and literature."   *Ibid.*

Continues the same author in a foot-note: "Diodorus relates, that the Egyptians learned the custom of deifying their kings from the Ethiopians; nay, according to him, the Egyptians derived statuary, and even their letters themselves, from the same source.   This author also observes, that the Egyptian and Ethiopian priests, as well as kings, wore caps, wreathed round with serpents, called asps, by which was intimated that every person guilty of treason would as certainly suffer death as if he had been bit by that poisonous animal."

The progress of Cush into the interior toward the Niger, was comparatively easy, because having no opposing foe or people to resist, but simply an unsettled country before him, he was, undoubtedly, the pioneer in the peopling and settlements of communities in Africa, and all Soudan and Nigratia now teem with the millions of his descendants.

Our subject is the "Origin of Races and Color," and our present theme the "Progress of the African Race;" hence, we shall closely confine ourselves to what pertains to the original settlers, Ham and his sons, without regard to their successors who, centuries after, succeeded them in the persons of the descendants of Shem and Japheth, to usurp their places and imitate their greatness.

CHAPTER X.

BUILDERS OF THE PYRAMIDS.

The Pyramids evidently are the very earliest, the oldest of the architectural structures in Egypt, commenced, no doubt, by the joint action of the first settlers under the three great rulers of the upper and lower Nile country, Ethiopia and Egypt, as sacred historical depositories of their bodies after death, as well, probably, also with scientific significance for astronomical and other purposes. It is said that, by certain geometrical calculation, they record mathematically the history of all time past to their erection. But of this there is nothing authentic.

The great Pyramid of Cheops was evidently designed for Ham, the Father Prince, and Cephenes for his successor of the sons, whichever followed him to the tomb. The third one in size for the son which followed last. To show the mathematical precision with which these structures were reared, it is said to have required one hundred thousand men twenty years to erect the first. By this it can be seen that one of any other given size after that, could be built in any given time. The form of these structures comports with the simplicity of the early period in which they were erected. The stone, cubic blocks, were modified and shaped to a cone (to use a paradox), which required an acquaintance with the science of conic sections and trigonometry. But they had it, whether by inspiration or acquirement, we know not, and need not care. There they stand to this day, "living monuments" of that race which first peopled that part of Africa.

The hieroglyphics among the earliest of their inventions, we shall next call attention to, as a department of their social polity. "We are informed by Diodorus Siculus, that the Ethiopians had anciently hieroglyphic characters as well as the Egyptians. Thus, among them, a hawk signified anything that made a quick dispatch, that bird in swiftness exceeding most others; the crocodile denotes malice; the eye, the maintainer of justice, and the guard of the body; the right hand, open, represented plenty; and the left, closed, a secure possession of property. But whether the Egyptians or Ethiopians first, in reality, hit upon this way of writing, cannot certainly be known, though Diodorus attributes the invention of it to the latter." *Ibid.*

We here introduce the hieroglyphics, the reading of which will be observed, accord to our version, or that which we obtained from study among the Africans themselves, by learning the significance or meaning of certain objects or things.

The reading of the first column or hieroglyphic paragraph, is thus rendered : " O, King, may thy soul (vital or never dying parts), as a boat upon the waters, run with thirst to God the fountain, everlasting Creator and Maker (or Builder) of all things, and all mankind " (men and women).

Had the bird a disc of the sun over it thus: then the meaning and significance would have been very different, and read: "O ! King, son of a king (son of one who had been a king), the son of a king, may thy soul attain," etc.

The reading of the second column or paragraph, is thus to be rendered : " O ! ever watchful eye, Thy name shall run and be handled as a boat upon the *water*, stand firm as the *pillars* of heaven, as long as *water* and *land* (earth) and *all things* under heaven and earth (all other things) exist, standing with *time* as *solid* as a *rock* above the *waters*, while the *sun* continues to shine."

By closely comparing the words *italicized*, in regular order with the emblems, it will be seen that these hieroglyphics are comprehensible by study, and beautifully illustrative of the philosophy of those illustrious ancient Africans, to whom the age is indebted for the propagation of that glorious light of progressive civilization—religion, philosophy, arts, science and literature in general, which now illuminate the world. To illustrate some of these curious linguistic symbols, take, for example, the figure the outlines of the eye; hence, a representation of God. Also, the picture of an owl—always an ominous bird—standing near a water-pot, by which it is conjectured that nothing could have induced so cautious a creature to approach but thirst.

And the representation of a man building the wall of a city, and other things next below it; and lastly a mer-man and mer-maid, or part man-fish and part woman-fish, with other things below them; the peculiar horse head-like figure, also represent-ing God—Khuam—will almost give a key to the whole system.

These hieroglyphics are copied from the obelisks of Luxor, taken by Champollion from Egypt to Paris, where they are now deposited as relics of antiquity.

| His translation of the first column is thus rendered: "Thy name is as firm as heaven; the duration of thy days (is as) the disc of the sun."

That of the second column, thus: "May thy soul attain to Khuam (spirit of God, one of the forms of Ammon the Creator) the Creator of all mankind (literally man and woman)."

This is claimed by Champollion to be a record of Rameses III. as Sesostris. Rameses II. from all the facts of history, we think much more reconcilable with that of the person of Sesos-tris. Ham as we have shown was Jupiter Ammon and Rameses I. he being the first ruler in Egypt, while Cush his eldest son, settled on the upper Nile, establishing the Kingdom of Ethiopia, and Mizraim in Midian. But Mizraim left the land of Midian, and joining his father, ruled jointly with him as a sub-ruler, when succeeding to the throne of Egypt after the death of Ham, he be-came Rameses II. and consequently must have been Sesostris.

One fact in the hieroglyphical record seems to settle the identity of the persons and periods of their rule in Egypt.

The figure thus:
son;" which signifies
who was the son of a
of the first inscrip-
column, instead
this:
figure I
that the
son of
indica-
first of

is read, "Son, son of a
a king, the son of a king,
king. But in the case
tion of the Luxor
of that, we have
the same symbol with a unit or
(one) above it, which implies
prince it represents was not the
a prince who ruled in that country,
ting this prince himself to be the
his line who ruled. We think

from this it is plain, that the Luxor inscription cannot refer to Rameses III. as instead of I (one) above the bird which represents a phœnix, it should have been the disc of the sun: had it represented the dynastic successor of a ruler. This

important fact must also be remembered, that in addition to
the sun-disc over the phœnix,
the symbol of the country over
which he ruled must be placed
under it thus:
showing that he ruled over
that country.

We think that it is plain, instead of the interpretation of Champollion, that the inscription on the left hand column of the obelisk of Luxor, now deposited in France, as being in commemoration of Rameses III. it is none other than Rameses I. Ham, or Jupiter Ammon.

As strikingly establishing the Ham line of the Rameses dynasty, and of great importance to the student of Ethiopian and Egyptian archæology, we call attention to the fact, that this important relation in the princehood of "Son of a Son," in the rule of sovereigns is not to be met with in history, except in that of the two kingdoms now under consideration. Of the four sons of Ham, three are known to have gone into Africa, Canaan alone remaining in Asia. This family then became famous throughout all the regions round about as rulers, warriors and conquerors, and Ham himself having been at the head, "The Sons" would have been the most easy and definite distinction in alluding to them, during the entire period of the Ham line dynasty.

But it may be said that this singular distinction or designation of a prince, "Son of a Son," was found to have existed in long periods after the Rameses dynasty, even among the Pharaohs. This may be true; and is it any wonder that the dynasty of the Rameses should be copied or imitated by those who came after? In the dynasty of the Pharaohs has been found the Assyrian, as we read in the Scriptures the complaint of the Israelites in Egypt, "the Assyrian has oppressed us." As Nimrod, the grandson of Ham, was the founder of the Assyrian Empire, may we not in this find a solution to the "Son of a Son," being found in the dynasty of the Pharaohs? We think the problem in this is solved, and that the princehood of a "Son of a Son" clearly belongs to the line of Ham.

CHAPTER XI.

PROGRESS IN LITERATURE.

"Lucian makes the Ethiopians to have excelled all other nations in wisdom and literature." And, continues Cummings Antiquities : "*Heliodorus* says, that the *Ethiopians* had two sorts of letters, the one called *regal*, the other *vulgar*; and that the regal resembled the *sacerdotal* characters of the *Egyptians*."

We have already treated upon that first branch of their literature, hieroglyphics, under the head of Builders of the Pyramids, and we add here, that according to Lucian, "they invented astronomy and astrology, and communicated those sciences, as well as other branches of learning, to the Egyptians. As their country was very fit for making celestial observations, such a notion seems not entirely groundless, though scarce any particulars of their knowledge had reached us."

We present here, copied from Cummings, taken from the great History of Ethiopia by that learned Israelite in Ethiopian literature, Job Ludolphus, the *regal* letters or Royal Ethiopian Alphabet, which none but the kings, priests, royal family and nobility were expected to learn.

The hieroglyphics were the vulgar or common letters, because representing objects or things to the eye, known and understood at sight by the common people, the composition or combination of which into sentences, could easily be learned by them. Hence, a hawk, for swiftness, meant dispatch or hasty news; a crocodile, for its meanness, meant malice; a serpent, danger; the open right hand, plenty; the closed left hand, safety or security: a jackal, watchfulness or vigilance; an oxen, patience; a sheep, innocence or harmlessness; a dove, love and innocence; a pigeon, news sent abroad; a swallow, news received; a rat or rabbit, caution, to be aware from their ruining habits; a water jug, thirst; the eye, Divine watchfulness, all-seeing; water, to run as a stream; land or territory, a country, ⬛⬛ representing hills and dales, an owl, always ominous and portentious; a dog, friendship, fidelity, faithfulness and trustworthiness; and a cat, constant companionship, meekness and constancy; a cock, boast or banter; a horse and chariot, preparation for war; all of which readily address themselves to the senses and comprehension of the common people.

The hieroglyphics are letters forming a literature founded upon the philosophy of nature without an alphabet; but that which we shall now present is of a much higher order, being artificial characters based on metaphysical philosophy of language.

THE OLD ORIGINAL ETHIOPIAN ALPHABET.

𐌰 *Alf.*	H *Zai.*	⌒ *Mai.*	Φ *Kof.*
Ω *Bet.*	Z *Hbarm.*	Z *Nabas.*	Z *Rees.*
2 *Geml.*	ᛗ *Tait.*	Ⅱ *Saat.*	W *Saut.*
ℛ *Dent.*	P *Jaman.*	▽ *Ain.*	✝ *Tawi.*
𐌼 *Haut.*	𝑛 *Caf.*	Z *Af.*	
Φ *Waw:*	Λ *Lawi.*	ℛ *Tzadai.*	

With our limited knowledge in archiology, we have always believed that the philosophy and root of alphabetical literature had its origin in Africa, or with the Hamite family. We have gone a step aside from this, and claimed that the first sixteen letters of the Greek alphabet, from *alpha* A to *pi* II, originated in Africa, as a part of the sacerdotal alphabet, the Greeks adding eight more, from *ro* P to *omega* Ω.

We call attention to the Ethiopian alphabet presented on page 53, the oldest, we believe, on record, if we discard the extraordinary assertion of Confucius, the Chinese historian, who claims for his race a civilization and literature fifteen thousand years older than the theological period of creation. But happily for our claim, we believe they have no alphabetical arrangement.

The second Ethiopian *Bet.* Ω, gives the twentieth Greek *upsilon* U, small, a little modified, inverted; the fifth *Haut* gives the twenty-first Greek *Psi* Ψ modified; seventh *Zai* H gives *eta* H, the seventh Greek; the eighth Ethiopian *Hbam* gives the fourteenth Greek *zi* ξ modified; the tenth *Lawi* Λ, gives *lambda* Λ, the eleventh Greek; the fifteenth *Saat* Π gives *pi* Π, the sixteenth Greek, modified; the sixteenth *Ain* ∇ gives *delta* Δ the fourth Greek, inverted; the nineteenth *Kob* Φ gives *phi* Φ the twenty-first Greek; the twentieth *Rees* Z, gives *zeta* Z, the sixth Greek; the twenty-first *Saut* ω gives small *omega* ω, the fifteenth Greek; the twenty-fourth *Tawi* T, gives *tau* T, the nineteenth Greek, modified. There is a slight modification in several of the letters, but the essential structure of the character is the same in both.

We regard the comparison of much importance in such a work as this, upon a most interesting subject to the whole human family.

And we must here beg to be borne with when we record our conviction that the literature of the Israelites, both in the science of letters and government, also religion, was derived from the Africans, as they must have carried with them the civilization of those peoples and that country, in their memorable exodus, as the highest encomium upon Moses in the Scripture is, that he " was learned in all the wisdom of the Egyptians." Of their religion and laws, we shall treat in another place.

They "invented Astronomy and Astrology," says Lucian.

And this important fact, however much it may be doubted by those who have given little or no thought to the subject, is borne out by the arrangement of this department of science, as the constellations beautifully illustrate. We shall designate the principal constellations having a direct bearing upon the subject, according to the legend of astronomical history: Cepheus and Cassiopea, Andromeda and Perseus, Pegassus and Cetus: the king and queen of Ethiopia, their daughter and son-in-law, the horse which carried them (the son-in-law and daughter) to heaven, and the monster of the sea which approached the shore of Ethiopia to destroy the Princess while taking a surf bath, when she was saved by Perseus who was watching her, and slew the monster and escaped to heaven on the winged horse. Orion and Auriga, beautiful constellations, are none other than Nimrod and Rameses II. and Sirius, is none other than Osiris.

And all these important facts seem to have been lost sight of, or passed unnoticed, by those who dispute so high a civilization as this given to the Ethiopians at so early a day, as being the authors of astronomical science. And do not these facts of those people comport with the living reality of their knowledge of the science of geometry, by the existence of those monuments of mathematical accuracy, the " everlasting Pyramids" ?

What power brought to the plains of Egypt, through sand and bog, from no one knows where, shaped, lifted and placed those great cubic rocks of many thousand tons weight, one above the other in regular and symmetrical layers to a given height, decreasing from the first surface layer, finishing by a cap stone, large enough for from twenty to forty persons to stand upon, but a knowledge of mathematics?   None other whatever.

And, doubtless, it was dwelling among and studying, in after ages, the structure of these great monuments, that induced Euclid to pursue his mathematical studies to the discovery of the forty-seventh problem, which seems to be the *ne plus ultra* or termination of problems in that science, as none beyond it has since been discovered.

CHAPTER XII.

THEIR RELIGIOUS POLITY.

The religious polity of the Ethiopians and Egyptians was splendid, indeed; and we shall treat of that of both of these peoples together, as that of one was that of the other, and though the religion was much older than the literature, as was that of all other peoples perhaps, we have, on account of its grandeur, preferred to place it second in the progress of African civilization.

They believed in one omnipotent God, who ruled over all things, possessing three distinct personal attributes, and always so represented Him. They also believed in a Mediator, through whom alone they could approach God; but their Kings were their mediatorial deities, through whom alone God answered all their desires, and their Priests, tutelary divinities, by whom the desires of the people were made known to the gods or kings. Though they recognized the personality of one true God, they always represented Him in three distinct persons; indeed, their idea of His personality was that of a Three-One-God.

This was most beautifully exemplified and illustrated in the person of Ham, Rameses I. deified and worshipped as Jupiter Ammon. He was represented as the body of a man, with the head of a ram with handsomely curved, extended horns, seated on a great white throne of gold and ivory; in his left hand he held a golden wand or sceptre, and in his right a thunder-bolt; at his right side sat a phœnix with extended wings, generally mistaken for and called by writers an eagle—the Greeks having first given rise to this mistake by representing their Jupiter attended by an eagle, in imitation of Jupiter Ammon by a phœnix.

How symbolical is this representation from the throne to the God-head—gold for purity; ivory for durability; the sceptre for authority, and thunder-bolt for power. And how figurative the ram's head. A sheep for harmlessness or innocence; yet a caution or admonition not to approach too near, illustrating the biblical declaration, that "no man can look upon God's face and live;" as it is a fact, that anything, man or beast, whose head approaches that of a ram's, is instantly met with a terrible butt. And the phœnix, how marvellously illustrative of the essential attributes of the Christian's conception of God, as a self-created being, without beginning or end.

The Phœnix, by the legend, was a bird that lived in Africa ; there never was but one, which never had a beginning nor an end, but transfigurated and renewed itself at illimitable periods of time—a large and stately bird, resembling an eagle, much larger and handsomer in symmetry of form and beauty of plumage.   Color, a beautiful pea-green, bright golden wings and golden tail, a solid crest of gold upon its head, and brilliant green cape-feathers, with a breast of gold.   It always walked and never flew, and was never known to eat or drink, and kept secluded from all living things.   It lived and lived on through ages and periods, and periods and ages of time, for hundreds of thousands of years; when seeming weary of life, it commenced to build a nest of sticks and broken limbs of trees gathered in the forest, which consumed a long period of time in con-struction.   When, in course of time, the nest was finished, the phœnix sat upon it about the same length of time it required in construction, when it dropped a golden egg, which instantly set the nest in a flame of fire; then raising up in excitement its head and wings, it, together with the nest, was consumed,· leaving nothing but a heap of whitish ashes, in which was found a round ball, out of which a white worm worked itself, which instantly sprang into a full-sized phœnix.   Such is the beautiful legend, as the history of this allegorical bird, one of the symbols of the Deity as understood by Ethiopia and Egypt.   Here, again, is the beautiful scriptural illustration of a "self-created God," and " our God is a consuming fire," the " worm that never dieth."

Again, Ham, the father, was Rameses I.   Jupiter Ammon, represented as a sheep or ram ; Mizraim, a son, joint ruler and successor, was Rameses II.   Sesostris, represented as Apis, an ox or bull ; Kush or Cush, the eldest son, co-joint ruler in the upper Nile region in Egypt, and master ruler in Ethiopia and Meroe, was, by courtesy of family pride and dynastic policy, called Rameses III. ; Osiris, represented as a dog. Hence, in the genius of Ethiopian and Egyptian polity, these three great princes became inseparably united into one god-head, of a father and two sons, or three persons in one, as Rameses, Sesostris and Osiris; the sheep, ox and dog, or ram, bull, dog. The dog is sometimes represented as a jackal, especially when in the attitude of guardianship or vigilance. Hence, from that period, the god or gods of Ethiopia and Egypt, were represented as three persons in one. And here, again, we see that the golden calf set up and worshipped by the Israelites in the wilderness, was in imitation of the bull-god of Egypt, and so was the Saviour who spent the first twelve years of his life in Egypt, called the " Lamb of God," no doubt in remembrance of the ram-god, revered for his goodness and innocence, the people there at that time being in sympathy with the " young child and his mother."

There was another striking metaphysical conception in the persons of these Ethiopian and Egyptian gods: the wealth of the country, and watchful care of the Almighty, in the character of the gods themselves. As stock in cattle comprised the greater part of the wealth of oriental countries in those days, two of the persons of the Three-One-God consisted of the most valuable cattle stock, bovine and sheep; one was of a guardian nature, canine, a dog, to watch and guard them. A most beautiful and wonderful conception was all this religious polity of theirs, from beginning to end. Conceptions such as these could only have emanated from the minds and morals of a people of the highest susceptibility and progressive civilization.

CHAPTER XIII.

WHO WERE THE GODS.

To determine the race representatives of the Egyptian gods, will go far toward deciding the disputed questions as to who were the first inhabitants of Egypt and builders of the pyramids, catacombs and sphinxes. Who were the people in so remote a period susceptible of such intellectual development as to capacitate them for such a work? As says the Duke of Argyll, in his able dissertation on the original development of human faculties: "In any case we may safely assume that Man must have begun his course in some one or more of these portions of the earth, which are genial in climate, rich in natural fruits, capable of yielding the most abundant return to the very simplest act. It is under such conditions that the first establishment of the human race can be easily understood; nay, it is under such conditions only that it is conceivable at all, and as these are the conditions which would favor the first establishment, and most rapid increase of Man, so also are these the conditions under which knowledge would most rapidly accumulate, and the earliest possibilities of material civilization would arise." And at last, and for once, we have the admission from a highly cultivated, able, eminent and popular author, that such a climate as that of the country upon which we are now treating—Africa, the land of our fathers—is favorable to rapid intellectual development, and the advancement of progressive civilization. And how true is this! It has long been known to the natural scientist that Africa, as a continent, excels all others in natural productions: animal, vegetable and mineral. That its fauna and flora are the most profuse

and best developed of any quarter of the globe; indeed, so far
from stupefying and depressing, as popularly taught in our school-
books, the climate and inhalations of the aroma and odors with
which the atmosphere is impregnated, are exciting causes, favorable to intellectual development. No intellect is more active,
nor perception more acute, than that of the native African. He
is all life, all activity, all device; and during his earliest period
of propagation and progress of civilization, must have been fully
equal to the requirements and demands of the times.

In addition to the mythological characters assigned the three
great Kings—father and two sons—Rameses I. Ham as Jupiter
Ammon, Rameses II. Mizraim as Sesostris, and Rameses III.
Cush as Osiris; inseparably united as three great columns support-
ing an edifice as Rameses, Sesostris and Osiris—the ram, bull
and dog—the auspicious conception in the ideal character of the
last representation is peace, patience and friendship. The sheep
for peace, ox for patience, and dog for friendship. Besides the
characteristic of peace, the sheep supplies wool, horns, hide,
flesh and tallow, for food and commerce; the ox the same, besides his utility as a working animal, and the milk of cows;
hence, the basis of wealth in these countries; and from his faithfulness and usefulness to man, the dog was justly entitled to a
representation as one of the gods, under whose auspices the people placed themselves. Hence, the account in classic history,
informing us that "the Egyptians once elected a Dog for their
King." We can well understand that this idea originated in an
allegorical representation, in the dog, of Cush as King of Egypt.
What a magnificent conception in these Three-One-Gods of
peace, patience and friendship. And this conception was born
of Ethiopia, as we shall show. But this is just the point in dis-

pute by most modern writers who pretend any acquaintance with
the hisory of the ancient inhabitants of the valley of the Nile.

And even that masterly, popular writer whose work on natural science, the "Reign of Law," is so much admired as a most
valuable contribution to sterling literature—we mean the Lord of
Argyll—flounders and staggers at this point. Says his Grace the
Duke: "There is a point at which the evidence of archæology
begins before the evidence of history closed.   There is border
land where both kinds of evidence are found together, or rather
where some testimony exists of which it is difficult to say whether it is the testimony of written documents or the inarticulate
monuments of man.   It was the habit of one of the most ancient
nations in the world, to record all events in the form of pictorial
representations.   Their domestic habits, their foreign wars, their
religious beliefs, are thus all presented to the eye."   His Grace
continues: "In one of the most perfect of the paintings which
have been presented to us, a great Egyptian monarch is symbol-
ically represented as ruling with the power of life and death over
subject races; and these are depicted with accurate and characteristic likeness. Conspicuous in the group is one figure, painted
to the life both in form and color, which proves that the race
which departs most widely from the European type, had acquired
exactly the same characters which mark it in the present day.
The Negro kneels at the feet of Sethos I. in the same attitude of
bondage and submission which typifies only too faithfully the
enduring servitude of his race.   The blackness of his color, the
woolliness of his hair, the flatness of his nose, the projection of
the lips, which are so familiar to us all—all these had been fully
established and developed thus early in the known history of the

world.   And this was about 1400 years before the Christian era
—that is to say, more than 3500 years ago.''

Why place so much stress on this one single black figure
among the group of ''subject races''?   If Sethos were a mighty
monarch and had subjugated Egypt and Ethiopia with other
races, certainly it might reasonably be expected that they would
be represented in the subject group.   But his Lordship is emphat-
ic in the statement, that ''conspicuous in this group is one figure
(and only one) painted to the life, both in form and color.''
The very prominence in which was placed that figure, shows the
estimated importance attached to such a subjugation by Sethos,
and that the race which the Negro in the kneeling group represented, was a people who esteemed themselves above subjugation.   The Negro of the group was a representative of the race
who inhabited and ruled in Egypt and Ethiopia; and hence the
importance attached to him as a captive subject at the feet of
Sethos.

'' I am informed by Professor Lepsius (through the kindness
of Mr. Poole),'' continues the Duke, '' that there are some still
earlier representations of the negro referable to the 'twelfth
dynasty,' or to about 1900, B. C.   And of this a further proof
is to be found in the fact, that at a period at least 2000 years
B. C., that is about the time of Abraham, mention is made in
hieroglyphic writing of black or negro troops being raised by an
Egyptian king to assist him in the prosecution of a great war.''

In illustration of this, an excellent elaborate drawing is
given as a frontispiece to '' Primeval Man '' by the Duke, to
which he refers in a foot-note, page 102:   '' Drawings by the
skilful hands of Mr. Bonomi are given on p. 101, and on frontispiece in illustration of the facts stated in the text.   They are

taken from an Egyptian temple at Beyt-el-Welee, in Nubia, of the reign of Rameses II. son and successor of Sethos I."

Why should an Egyptian king be raising negro troops to prosecute a great war, if the negro race was an abject people at that time, as herein intimated; and why not raise troops from other races in the kingdom, if the negro race did not comprise the inhabitants of Egypt? What was an Egyptian temple doing in Nubia? Nubia certainly is not Egypt, nor any part of it, but was anciently a part of Ethiopia. These are questions looking to the settlement of an important ethnological enquiry.

Nor is this all. For, while on the very text in reference to the "Negro kneeling at the feet of Sethos in the same attitude of bondage and submission which typifies too faithfully the enduring servitude of his race," his Grace, as if in contradiction of what he had just indited, says: "Nor is this the whole evidence afforded by the Egyptian pictures. At periods not much later in history, we have elaborate representations of battles with Negro nations, representations which go far to show that the race was then more able to maintain a contest with other races than it has ever been in recent times." This admission of the hieroglyphic representations to be found on the temples and monuments of Egypt of the advanced status of the negro race, settles at once the controversy, and leaves only to be proven the fact, that the earliest settlers, builders of the pyramids, sculptors of the sphinxes, and original god-kings, were blacks of the negro race.

Examine the pictures taken from the frontispiece of "Primeval man," and what do we see? As his Grace explains, p. 102, the drawings are taken from an Egyptian temple at Beyt-el-Welee, in Nubia, of the reign of Rameses II. And what is

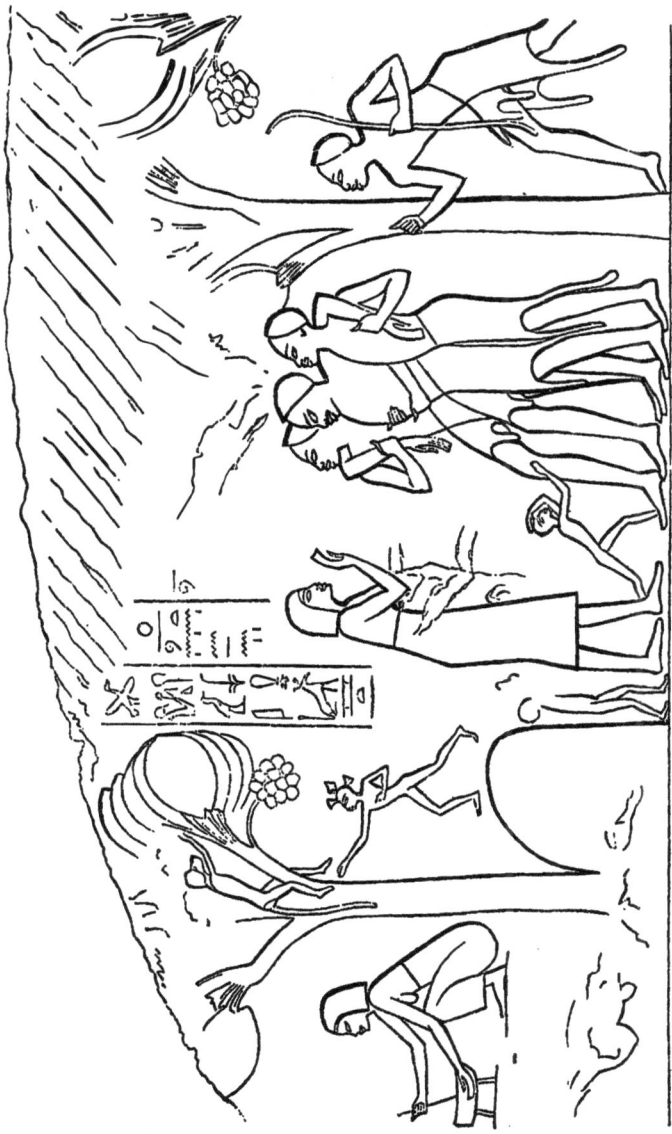

See Page 64.

Bonomi Del

this representation ?   We are told that it is the obtaining of black troops for the army of Rameses.   Nor is that all ; it is more, as the hieroglyphics and parts of the figures unmistakably show.

The three persons thus linked together, are of the priesthood, high in rank, who, in the position and order of recruited or conscript soldiers, present themselves before a priestess of the goddess Isis, who represents to them that the requirements of the king are plentiful, the country or kingdom is safe, and good news shall ever precede or go before him.   The back figure in the rear of the three priests representing soldiers, who is also a priest, stands at a respectful distance, giving a divine or royal salutation ; the little nude figure immediately in front of the priestess, shows the status or character of the three men by the homage which it pays them with the reverential salutation.   And the little female figure immediately behind her, is an attendant on her sacredness.

The female squatting at a vessel is a priestess, who holds the handle of an implement, a spoon or a ladle, in her right hand, while the left is open, palm upwards, aside the vessel, indicating to the priests that the goddess has decreed a plentiful supply of provisions.   In the column of hieroglyphics—for the Ethiopians and Egyptians read as we do, from left to right—at the top a pigeon is in flight, bearing good news to the king and army, while at the bottom is a jackal or dog, representing Osiris, the guardian of their possessions ; beneath it ⊐_____⊏, bars indicating security.   The second column reads, that the kingdom, though much disturbed by commotion, will stand as durable as the sun.   The sportive figure, with the dog-faced ape climbing a tree, is nothing but a harlequin or mountebank of the priesthood, a merry Andrew as diversion for the sacred order during leisure moments.

Another important representation. These three priests, while presenting themselves on behalf of their Sovereign as military vicars, imploring the favor of the gods, come in the three-one character of Rameses, Sesostris and Osiris—the ram, bull and dog—the gods themselves: the central as an old man, being supported by the other two—one on either side—Ham, Cush and Mizraim, the father and two sons. And each and every one of these human figures, from the mountebank to the priesthood, represent the Ethiopian race of the Negro type.

And yet we are told by his Lordship, that "the Negro knows no higher position even to this day, than to kneel at the feet of Sethos, in utter servitude." Would the priesthood, who among them in those days were always of the royal stock and nobility, be chosen from the Negro race, if that race had only been subordinate and thus degraded? Would the whole group of people represented on those pillars at Beyt-el-Welee, in Nubia, have been of the race of any other people than those who designed and placed them there? No such thing. And the fact is, that the Negro race comprised the whole native population and ruling people of the upper and lower region of the Nile—Ethiopia and Egypt—excepting those who came by foreign invasion; and the entirety of the Negro group in this important historical representation, can be readily accounted for from the fact of the columns being found in Ethiopia, a part of this country—Africa—where foreigners did not so frequently reach, and therefore did not deface and erace, as was common in regard to those for centuries found in Egypt.

The successive invaders of Egypt were Assyrians, Persians, Greeks, Macedonians, Romans and Saracens, till modern times brought us down to the Arabs and Turks. And what now is erroneously called the remnants of the ancient Egyptian race— Copts and Berbers—are nothing more than a mixed race, the descendants of the original inhabitants, the Ethiopian or Negro race and Saracens, the last successful invaders and occupants of the country; they who burnt and destroyed the great Alexandrian Museum. That is what these Copts and Berbers are, and nothing more.

Is it still disputed, still doubted that the original inhabitants and native rulers of the countries of Ethiopia and Egypt were identical—blacks of the Negro race? Let it be remembered that every successive race which conquered those countries, made spoliations their first object, destroying as far as possible, the evidences of the greatness of those whom they conquered, especially their monuments, statuary, paintings and inscriptions, placing instead their own designs, claiming, as far as successfully could be done, for their own that which should have been placed to the credit of the vanquished. Hence, the general absence of the evidence of African greatness where it should be found, and that of those who succeeded to power and rule in their stead. Thus we see Cleopatra's Needle, Pompey's Pillars, the Alexandrian Museum, and other evidence of foreign designs, while the truly African is destroyed or carried away to Rome and Greece, in ancient, and France and Britain, in modern times. On this subject, Mr. Rollin, the historian, exclaims: "The Romans, despairing to equal the Africans in greatness, thought it honor enough to borrow the monuments, statues and paintings of their kings and great men." And Champollion, at a comparatively recent date, found, fallen where it had been dashed down upon its face, doubtless by invading ravagers long years before, the statue of Rameses, which at great expense and trouble, he had removed to France. All these are facts showing how evidence of African greatness has been designedly taken away and destroyed. And who that has seen, at the Crystal Palace, Sydenham, near London, England, the reproduction of the statues of those three famous Egyptian personages—Rameses, Sesostris and Osiris—as they sat as the main pillars of a temple, but was struck with their very African features of cheek bones, great white eyes, wide nostrils, broad mouths and gibbous lips?

And if every other evidence in archæology had failed to establish the identity of the Ethiopian of the Negro race, with that of the original Egyptian in his highest civilization, there is yet *one* which never has been destroyed nor defaced, but, like the "everlasting pyramids," has stood through all time to the present, silently, though most eloquently, pleading the identity of the African race of the Negro type with that of the original inhabitants of the upper and lower Nile, known as Ethiopia and Egypt. Asia had her ideal genius of race representation in *Asiatica;* Europe in *Europa,* and America, in modern days, in her *America,* or Goddess of Liberty ; but we ask, in all reason and soberness, whether any other race than the African in the symbolical representation of the Sphinxes, would have placed the great head of a *Negro woman* on the body of a lion or lioness, as it may be, as the ideal representative of the *genius* of their *race?* None other, especially as we know by archæology that the Sphinxes represented the Queens of Egypt through different dynasties. This settles indisputably and forever, we think, this question of the original race inhabitants of the Nilotic regions of Africa.

And we call attention to another fact, useful and important, we think, as a hieroglyphical record, which is that the inscription copied from "Primeval Man," as coming from the Nubian Temple, relates to a woman and not to a man. Isis was regarded as the moon, and Osiris as the sun ; hence, ☉ (sun) represented a king, and ◯ (moon), a queen. The difference in the figure simply being a small circle in the centre of the disk of the sun, thus : ◉ or dot, thus : ☉ and the moon having a clear disk, thus : ◯ . Female royalty without sovereignty, or a high priestess, is frequently represented in hieroglyphical texts, thus : ◠ as a half moon, but seldom, if ever, as a crescent, thus : ☾ ; as this has always an astronomical significance, it should be observed that the flat side of the disk or semicircle, is always turned down.

As the text here given in hieroglyphics ends in the first column with ◠ , and in the second column commences with the ◯ ; it is very apparent that it relates to the sacred offices and high royal position of a woman. And as Sethos or Sethon was said to have been a priest of Vulcan before becoming a king of Egypt, the ministering priestess, before whom stand the vicar soldier-priests, is none other than the High Priestess and Sovereign Queen of Egypt, the wife of Sethos or Sethon I., King of Egypt, as he is herein represented to be. And look at that profile—side face—and head dress, how perfectly sphinx-like it is. This is our reading and interpretation of the whole hieroglyphical inscription.

We have in a foregoing chapter given the color of the ram,

or sheep, representing Jupiter, as black ; so, also, was the bull, or ox, representing Apis, and the cow, or heifer, representing Isis, black.   The dog or jackal, representing Osiris, was also black.   And though some writers have mistakenly regarded Osiris as the ox or bull, it can, we think, never be disputed by students of ancient history and mythology, that Apis was the ox, a black bull, with a white star in his forehead.

CHAPTER XIV.

WISDOM OF ETHIOPIA AND EGYPT.

The mysterious allegory of the Garden of the Hesperides, we regard as the ultimate combined wisdom of Ethiopia and Egypt, comprising their ethics, religion, philosophy, literature, arts, science and wealth ; in a word, their entire social economy ; and that among the wreck of destruction consequent to the successive invasions and occupancy of these countries, especially Egypt, by foreigners, were these legends become as Lost Arts. Their reproduction was desirable, but not to be expected, and except by the most intimate intercourse with the native Africans of the highest intelligence in the interior, and assiduous study, could a conception be attained.

There is little doubt as to the Ethiopians having been the first people in propagating an advanced civilization in morals, religion, arts, science and literature—the Egyptians of the same race being co-operative, and probably co-ordinate.   Every fact in archæology and ancient research bears evidence of this.   The age of the Pyramids and masterly Sphinxes, from the peculiarity

of their characteristic structures, were among the earliest and
very first of their architectural works, and the only ones, from
their solidity, which have withstood the ravages and wreck of
time, and not been either entirely or partially destroyed by re-
moval, shattering, defacing or deforming.

We have proof, from very high authority of the antiquity
of the original rulers in Egypt—since as far back as the time of the
advent of the Israelites, the brethren of Joseph, into Egypt, B. C.
1706—that the dynasty of the Rameses had long since ceased,
and that of the Pharaohs was established, and a foreigner was on
the throne; for when Joseph presented his father as the representative head of his brethren before Pharaoh to ask permission to
settle them upon land, he said : "The land of Egypt is before
thee; in the best of the land make thy father and brethren to
dwell; in the land of Goshen let them dwell.

" And Joseph placed his father and his brethren, and gave
them a possession in the land of Egypt, in the best of the land,
in the land of Rameses, as Pharaoh had commanded." Gen.
xlvii. 6, 11.

Whatever may have been the length of time from their
advent into, till their exodus from, Egypt—and they dwelt there
upwards of four hundred years—it is evident to our mind that
the rule of the Assyrians continued during the Israelitish bondage. And when Abraham visited Egypt to escape a famine in
his own country, B. C. 1996, a Pharaoh ruled, and this was 2114
P. D., or after the deluge ; Nimrod having begun his reign in
Shinar, B. C. 2347. The advent of Kush and Mizraim into
Africa, must have been coeval with, if not anterior to, that of
Nimrod in his adventure; hence the antiquity of the first
original race rulers in Ethiopia and Egypt.

To recur to the past devastation of the Nilotic region by
invasion, and the consequent destruction of emblems, paintings,
statuary and designs, as well as other evidences of greatness of the
African race, we learn from authentic history, that when Cambyses, King of Persia, invaded Egypt, "he was so offended at
the superstition of the Egyptians, that he killed their god Apis—
the ox or sacred bull—and plundered their temples." And in
the history of the Ptolemies, we learn that when Ptolemy III.
surnamed *Evergetes*, returned from his oriental conquest,
"loaded with the spoils of nations, among the immense riches
which he brought he had above 2500—two thousand five hundred—Egyptian gods, which Cambyses had carried away into
Persia, when he conquered Egypt."

Think of this, by one conqueror; and what must have been
the spoliation and destruction by others before and since, during
a period of more than three thousand years! And yet, we still
expect to find evidence of their former greatness, by the remaining productions of the original inhabitants! It is simply im-
possible. We do know, that the first dynastic name in Egypt
was that of Rameses, and we claim that Ham himself was the
first who obtained it. And though his son Mizraim, who ruled
jointly with him, bore the name of Sesostris, he also took the
dynastic name of Rameses II. on succeeding his father to the
throne of Egypt. And for aught we know by history, the
dynastic title of Pharaoh first came by Assyrian succession in
Egypt. The Persian succeeded the Assyrian, but we do not
learn, as theirs was of comparative short duration, that they established a dynasty at all, and if so, what title, other than King
of Egypt, they bore. It may have been that, succeeding the

Pharaohs, they accepted of that regal title while holding the reins.

The Ptolemian dynasty was the next in succession to the Pharaoh, and of Greeko-Macedonian origin, as in another place stated, taking its rise on the division of the Macedonian Empire after the death of Alexander the Great, commencing with Ptolemais *Lagus,* nineteen years after the demise of Alexander, to whom, as one of the greatest and bravest of his generals, Egypt fell as his share of the empire. This dynasty was of long duration, continuing till B. C. 6.—six years before the advent of our Saviour Jesus Christ—and the last consequently of permanent foreign rule before the Christian era in Egypt. But we know that there were frequent irruptions and displacements among the several strong powers which succeeded to rule in Egypt and Ethiopia, as B. C. 640, Psalmaticus ruled, and previous to him, Sebachus, a powerful Ethiopian prince ascended the throne of Egypt, and ruled over both countries with great wisdom, prudence, moderation, and acceptance to the people. Also, as we learn, that B. C. 146, the Saracens made a descent upon and gained power in Egypt, which must have been during the Ptolemian dynasty, which for the time received a check, but resuming its power, continued till near the beginning of the Christian era, or within six years of that event.

Thus much we have said, in vindication of a race and people once enlightened, learned, proud and powerful, the leaders in civilization, whose status was such, that God, through his holy prophet, spake, saying : " And they shall be afraid and ashamed of Ethiopia their expectation, and Egypt their glory." Isa. xx. 6. This prophetic declaration shows not only the status, but the identity of race and international relations of these two peoples, whose every consideration has been looked upon and regarded in modern times as wrapped up in mystery, with uncertainty and doubt.

A historical circumstance recorded in Holy Writ, shows the height to which this race had attained, and the lasting influence shed abroad among the people as controlling their actions and conduct. Although their national power had passed away from them, their integrity and the virtue of their national polity were such, that when Herod, King of Judea, ordered the slaughter of the young children that the infant Saviour might be destroyed, "the angel of the Lord appeared to Joseph in a dream, saying, Arise, and take the young child and his mother, and flee into Egypt, and be thou there until I bring thee word; for Herod will seek the young child to destroy Him." Matt. ii. 13.

It must be remembered at this time, that the Romans as a nation held universal power over the other governments of the earth; that the Greeko-Macedonians ruled in Egypt, and both Jews and Greeks were subject to Roman power. All this seems wonderful and almost incredible, that only in Africa could the Son of God be saved. Nor is this all. God's purposes towards this race as made manifest, seems yet a higher destiny among the children of men. When Christ's mission on earth had been fulfilled, and the crucifixion decreed, as essential to the plan of salvation, according to the Christian belief, the Cross had to be borne up the hill of Calvary. Upon the shoulders of the Saviour it was placed three times, when he groaned and fell to the ground by reason of its weight. He could not bear it. "The spirit was willing, but the flesh was weak." Jews, Greeks, and Romans stood around, " who buffeted and scourged him " to compel him to carry it, but he could not; and they

would not do it, deeming it a disgrace to them to carry the cross
for his crucifixion. Under the cross the Son of God lay pros-
trate at the foot of Mount Calvary ! Here was a scene which
beggars description, and is almost sacrilegious to express; the
will of God thwarted, and the plan of salvation checked ! All
heaven might well have stood appalled, and angels gazed with
wonder, when just at this moment there appears at the scene "a
man of Cyrene, Simon by name (Simon *Niger*, meaning *black*
in the Latin tongue), him they compelled to bear his cross."
Matt. xxvii. 32. So the African was the first bearer of the
cross of Jesus Christ. Was this an accident, or a providence of
God? Was the ram caught by the horns in the bushes, as a
sacrifice for Abraham to save his son Isaac, an accident or a
providence of God ? If he thus provided for the salvation of
an individual, would he not also specially provide for the salvation of all mankind? We think this is beyond a question, and
prophetically designed. And yet another evidence of the favor
of Providence to this race, is presented in the Holy Scriptures.
After the mission of Christ had been completed, and the decree
went forth forbidding all people from following the believers and
teachers of His doctrine, Africa again appears in the person of
her sovereign, Queen of Ethiopia, who sends an ambassador to
Jerusalem to worship and be baptized in the Christian faith.
This person was the royal representative or commissioner from
Ethiopia, the chief treasurer to the Queen, who came in great
state, drawn in his chariot by camels, attended by a retinue of
followers. This is, probably, the first delegate ever sent to
receive the Christian religion for a nation. This nation was
black. Is not this wonderful ? Can we see no special providence in it ? Has God no purpose in all this ? Is there not in

this a prophetic destiny shown for this people, in a higher scale of morals and religion than has yet been attained? Being made the protectors of the infant Son of God; to assist in the plan of salvation; and, lastly, to promulgate the precepts of redemption taught by the ascended Saviour, certainly points to a higher and holier mission designed for that race than has yet been developed in the progress of civilization.

We now recur to that part of this chapter, the social polity of Ethiopia and Egypt, reduced to a legend of the Garden of the Hesperides. Such were their discretion, caution, prudence, judgment, care and jealousy of others, that whatever they desired to conceal, was exhibited in such a manner, that while it was perfectly plain and comprehensible to themselves, the design was obscure and unintelligible to others.

Take for example the figure (page 65) from the Duke's "Primeval Man," and while the three priests present themselves in the attitude of soldiers—and we know by their caps and dress that they are priests—before the high priestess or goddess, Isis, to beg divine favor for the King in raising troops, a special messenger-priest, as the representative of his majesty, stands in the back ground, quite out of their, but full in her, sight, while he with his right hand presents her with the royal salutation; he at the same time holds firmly in the grasp of the clinched fist of his left hand the emblem of a bow, to assure the priestess that she is not imposed upon, and will be safe in meeting the royal pleasure of the King, in any assurance she may make, or encouragement she may give to the persons before her. The national emblem was made to represent the power and strength of the country; in like manner was the second emblem made to represent the strength and power of the means and efforts represented by it as necessary in destroying all that is detrimental in promoting the highest civilization. And how beautifully illustrative are they, when reduced to an abridgment or condensed symbol.

The Garden of the Hesperides, as before stated, is an allegorical disguisement of the wisdom of the Ethiopians and Egyptians, a philosophical depository of the mental and material possessions of those countries, presented in one view to themselves, while concealed from others. And here is wherein consisted the beauties of their wisdom. The location of the garden has ever been to the historian as much of a mystery and a myth as the garden itself. Some supposed it to have existed in Egypt, others in Lybia, and some writers placed it in Northern Africa at the foot of the Atlas Mountains. But the Ethiopians themselves, the originators of the allegory, placed it, where most naturally it should have been, in Central Africa, where none had access to it but themselves. Then its contents, " golden fruits," the very words of which express everything of wealth, guarded by a dreadful dragon or serpent that never slept. What a place, and what a description of it! It is the concentrated view of such a place, as we believe to be among the lost arts of Africa, that we design here to reproduce—the national and family emblems, once the pride of Ethiopia and Egypt, the Garden of the Hesperides and place of its location, which we sacredly believe to have been none other than that region of Africa embracing the entire region of the Nile and Niger, especially including that mysterious portion now known as the Great Sahara, a place of untold wealth, of unequaled fertility and productiveness.

CHAPTER XV.

GARDEN OF THE HESPERIDES.

We present here this unique representation of the Garden of the Hesperides, a compendium of the domestic, social, moral, religious, literary, and political economy of Africa; in a word, the entire social science of those two peoples, Ethiopia and Egypt, epitomized, with no maudlin superstition, but conceived and couched in beautiful legendary tradition, handed down from the remotest period, with tender emotions and affectionate reminiscences of high regard for their great progenitors.

Explanations of all the deities with their attributes, will be found in the chapter on the religion of these people, which require no repetition here. As national and family emblems they have mottoes and precepts, and full notes of explanation are given.

1. PHŒNIX, motto: *Awa aton ato wawa* (we regenerate ourselves).

2. RAM, precept: *Alafia, lakari, ore* (peace, patience, friendship).

3. THUNDERBOLT, precept: *Imolli ti orun* (light from heaven).

4. GREAT SERPENT; first precept: *Aya odo* (wife of thunder, or river Niger, wife of river Nile. Second precept: *Ise-olorun ma-diyan* (fear not God's works).

5. PYRAMID; precept: *Bi-olorum pellu* (the Lord has been merciful to us).

SYMBOL OF THE GARDEN OF THE HESPERIDES.

See Page 80

The philosophy of Ethiopia and Egypt was replete with beautiful ethical instruction, the Garden of the Hesperides being a legendary or ideal consummation of their entire social polity; hence, the mottoes and precepts here given with this ideal compendium, are illustrative of the great original design of the legend—to inculcate ethics and religion. The hieroglyphical abridgments comprising the symbols here explained, are given in full, chap. x, page 46, with translation.

Next in order, we present an ideal symbol of the compendium of the progress of modern African civilization, designed to represent the moral, religious and physical aspect of the requirements and demands of the people and country of that continent; a land prolific with all the productions of the animal, vegetable and mineral kingdoms, pre-eminently excelling in flora and fauna all other quarters of the earth, yet behind and below all nations in the march and attainments of man.

Our compendium is designed to illustrate (unlike the Garden of the Hesperides) not what had been attained by great efforts and the high civilization of the ancient Africans, but that which is now required and demanded of the people of the present day of that race. A continent and race are to be redeemed and regenerated; this can only be accomplished by their own efforts, under the guidance of an all-wise Providence and His grace; and in addition, the aid of the civilization of the Christian nations of the earth should be tendered them.

This duty must be brought before the world, presented on a plan, in such a manner as to be appreciated by all Christian philanthropists, as part of the history and literature of the times in which they live. Every end must have a means adequate to its attainment; hence, the mighty work of the age of regenerating a race should have the favor of all modern civilization. To attain this, universal attention must be elicited. Hence, our object and method in presenting such a work as this. We proceed to an explanation of the symbol of modern civilization as shown on opposite page.

1. GIRAFFES, motto: *Nitilu* (the highest point), the same as excelsior.

2. GREAT HYDRA, precept: *Olorun tobi li obba* (God is the great King). Second precept: *Iroju li ohun gbo gbo* (perseverance is everything).

3. PHŒNIX, RAM and THUNDERBOLT: motto and precepts the same as given, except on the Ram in this symbol, when the precept *alafia* (peace) alone is given.

The modern compendium is a combination of a part of the ancient mythological symbols with modern, to facilitate the propagation of great principles underlying this mighty work of regeneration. The phœnix, ram and thunderbolt are now well understood to be of the ancient polity, but the four flaming torches in addition to the thunderbolt are of modern origin, and belong to the present people of Central Africa. The baton is called *ise* (club of Shango), and the blazing or burning end is called *owo ina* (flame of fire). These clubs of Shango always accompany the real head or skull bone with horns of a dead ram, and by the common people, especially those of passing caravans, are called "Shango torches." They are, doubtless, in this composition as now found in central Africa, the traditional symbolic representation of the ancient Jupiter Ammon ; hence the combination as here given.

A monster serpent—a two-headed hydra—is boldly placed in our pathway, sustained by dragons on either side entwined in

COMPENDIUM OF MODERN AFRICAN CIVILIZATION   *See Page 81*

its coils. This is a symbolic representation of the great river Niger, one head of which, doubtless, originates in the Kong Mountains, and another—that of the river Tchad, a tributary of the Niger—in the famous lake of the same name; the dragons representing the branches which flow in and strengthen the Niger along its entire course, presents itself in a dreadful and defiant attitude, as an obstacle to be subdued and utilized before our progress can be effective as central Africans.

A giraffe, in all ages a favorite among the ancients, and most innocent, delicate and timid of the wild animals, fearlessly attacks the dreaded monster on both sides, crushing beneath its feet the strengthening tributaries, symbolic of self exertion and perseverance; while in the centre stand the moral admonitions of the great work before us, symbolic of regeneration, guided by light from heaven, impelled by principles of peace, acknowledging only and trusting in God as the great King, who will safely lead us, encouraged by perseverance.

Thus are presented the ancient, the past, and prospective, that which is to and most assuredly will come, compendiums of our civilization.

All that is good and desirable in African polity and economy—and there is much for which they get no credit—we shall retain and endeavor to improve; and all that is good and desirable in the civilization of other races and peoples, we shall emulate and endeavor to profit by, and all that is demoralizing and objectionable in all races and peoples, of whatever degree of civilization, we shall reject in this our progress of civilization, as tending to degeneration, and thereby fatally pernicious to the desirable social polity.

CHAPTER XVI.

———

———

Surrounding the Garden of the Hesperides, is a monster resembling a serpent, at the end of whose tail is a bulb, and whose
head is triangular in shape; its nose above toward the upper angle;
eyes below the nose towards the mouth, from which the teeth
project the whole width along the lips.   This is in character
with the peculiarities of the Ethiopians and Egyptians, and with·
out explanation would be incomprehensible.

The garden, as previously explained, had reference to Central or Middle Africa, with its immense resources, inclusive from
the Mediterranean Sea to the Gulf of Guinea, or Sea of Ethiopia
as now called, all of which parts of the continent were well
known to them, especially the Ethiopians.

Around and about Egypt coursed in mysterious windings, the
Nile, the source of which was unknown, ending in the Mediterranean, with the Delta or peculiar triangular shaped mouths.

Around and about Central Africa and Southern Ethiopia—
now Nigratia—coursed the Niger (Aya) in the most remarkable
windings, whose source also was unknown, emptied into the Sea
of Ethiopia by thirteen streams or mouths, like its great co-ordinate territorial bounder, the Nile, making a triangular shaped ter-
minus or Delta.

By the ancient Africans, the Niger was called the "wife of
the Nile," (Odo, as it is called by the Yarubas,) and the Nile itself was called Thunder, supposed from the noise of its falls or
rapids as heard at certain seasons of the year.   And by mytho-

logical conclusions for political purposes, the two rivers were so regarded and said to be one; entwined around and protecting the interior riches of Africa, rising and falling to great heights and depths at different seasons of the year, they were represented and regarded as an immense sleepless Serpent which guarded the Garden of the Hesperides.

The bulb at the end of the tail is an imaginary lake, the source of the river; and the head is the Delta formed by the outlets; the teeth being shrubby growths fringing the shore at the outlets or mouths of the Niger and Nile; the eyes and nose, islands.

Outside of the serpent—our symbol—will be noticed the many water-plants and flowers, and various staple products, as palm-nut trees, dates, bananas, oranges, rice, corn, cotton, sugarcane, indigo, all products of the garden, but simply thrown on the outside to prevent derangement of the inside.

The appearance of the serpent is intended to represent the river at full tide, to the overflowing of the banks. What is true of the Nile is also the case with the Niger, near or about the same season of the year. Hence, the great plausibility of considering the two one. But since they were called and regarded husband and wife, they were mythologically and logically one. Hence, the precepts *Aya Odo*, an admonition of the extent of the garden and territory boundary guarded by the two-one serpent and the golden fruits therein contained. This, then, was the "Serpent which guarded the Garden of the Hesperides and protected the golden fruits thereof."

The pyramid at the entrance of the garden is represented as the "huge statue of Anteus," said to have been "overthrown" or "over-run" by Hercules, who "entered the garden and took possession of the golden fruits thereof;" the pine-apples at the lower part of the garden, as well as oranges and bananas outside of the serpent or stream, "being the golden fruits."

The language of all the mottoes and precepts is Egba or that spoken by the Yarubas, except the motto of the modern symbol at the heads of the giraffes—Nitilu—(pronounced on the short sound of *i* as in pin), which is Grebo, or that spoken by the Krumen of West Africa. Hence, the literature of the ancient symbol is composed of both ancient and modern, while that of the modern symbol is entirely modern African language.

CHAPTER XVII.

MODERN AND ANCIENT ETHIOPIA.

We may at this point be permitted to institute a comparison between the ancient and modern Ethiopians, the progenitors and descendants of the African race, by enquiring, What may be expected of the modern African, granting all that is claimed for the ancient, his progenitor?

We have seen the great susceptibility of the ancient Ethiopian in his adaptation to the highest civilization, to the extent of leading all other races in the stride of human progress. These in him were inherent faculties, designed by the Creator as essential to the Divine plan for the civilization of Man. Some race had to lead, to accomplish which the climate, soil, productions, scenery, external physical sensibilities and relative geographical location to the other races should be such as to enable them to impart and receive, with comparative facility, by communication with them. Such then was Africa, an eternal summer, "no

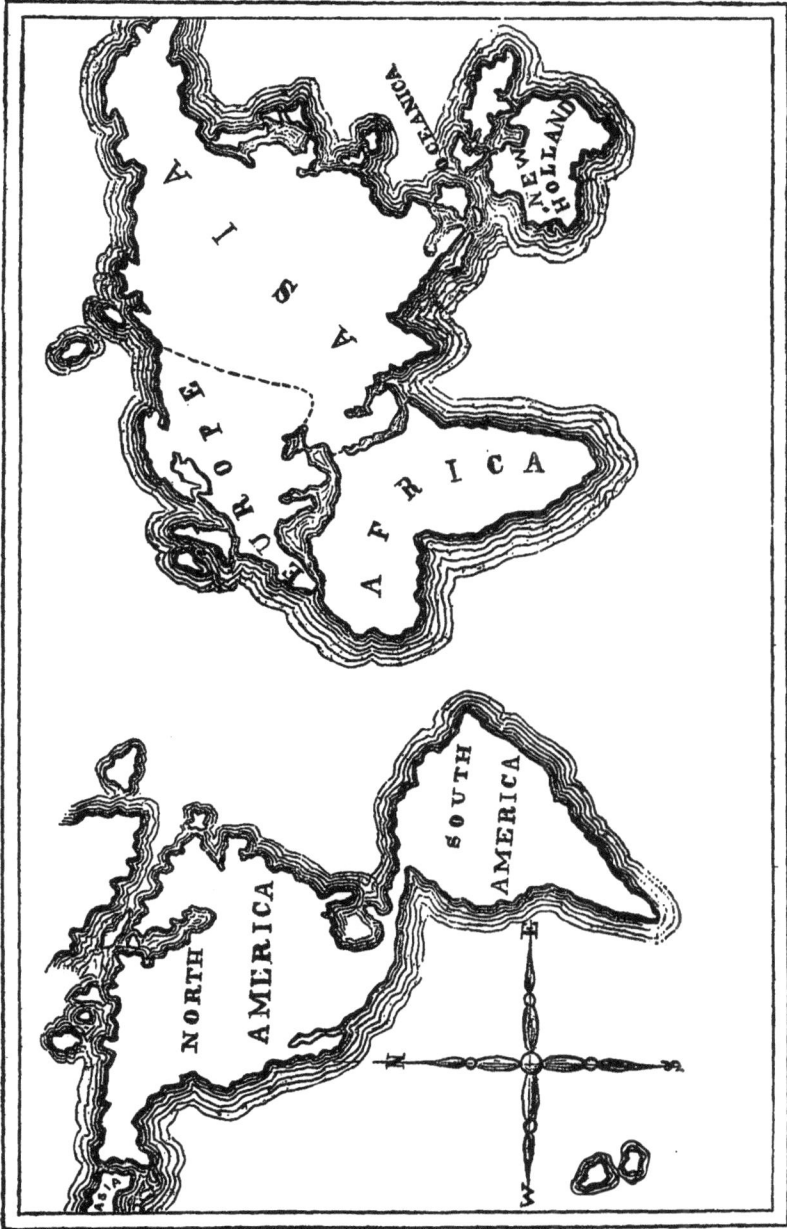

See Page 80.

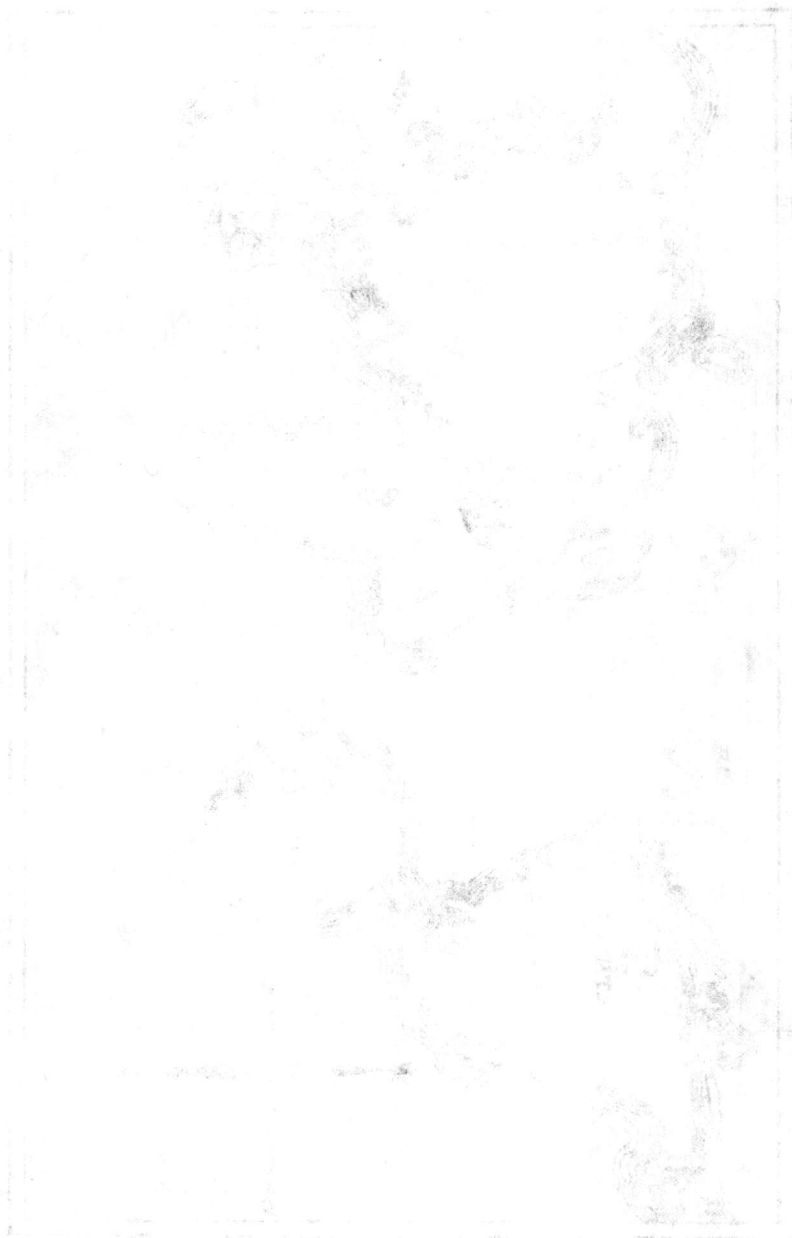

blighting frosts nor chilling winds," the most prolific and abundant productions of every kind, animal, vegetable and mineral. The landscape, scenery, beauty and odor of flowers, plumage and song of birds, and flavor of delicious fruits, all contributed to the external senses to the extent of continually reminding them of the certainty of an omnipotent God, the Creator of all things, on whom alone they at once placed their dependence.

Then again, in geographical location, Africa is the most remarkable in position. Look at the map of the world presented here on Mercator's projection, giving the face of the earth in its natural position, on a plane.

Of the five grand divisions of the globe, Africa stands in the centre. And in the old relation of these three first old divisions —without regard to America—we find Africa in the close proximate relation of being only separated from Europe by a disconnection of fifteen miles of water by the Straits of Gibraltar; and the closer relation of being joined to Asia by a connection of sixty miles of territory at the Isthmus of Suez. Such then were and are Africa's position and facilities for communication with the two other great races of man—the children of Shem and Japheth—and to us the most convincing evidence that in the earliest period of human progress, she and her children were made the centre and propagators of the highest civilization.

A remarkable characteristic of this race from the earliest period is " their high conception and reverence of a Creator of all things." This is indicated by the language they always used when speaking of God the Creator, as we understand and adore him.

We know of no other peoples or nations who had so high a conception of and reverence for God as the Ethiopians and

Egyptians, though they had many superstitions and also worshipped false gods—which were as matters of policy—and whatever profound metaphysical conception and sincere religious reverence the Israelites may have entertained and disseminated regarding the true God, they obtained both during their Egyptian bondage, and carried them from Egypt with them.

And the enquiry naturally presents itself: How do the Africans of the present day compare in morals and social polity with those of ancient times? We answer, that those south of the "Sahara," uncontaminated by influence of the coast, especially the Yarubas, are equal in susceptibility and moral integrity to the ancient Africans. Those people have all the finer elements of the highest civilization; virtue and matrimonial fidelity being the basis of female excellence and worth, and honor being held sacred among the men, their plighted word on their moral responsibility being a sufficiently binding obligation to ensure its fulfilment. Friendly, sociable and benevolent, they are universally the politest of people. Obscene, profane or blasphemous language is never heard among them, and quarrelling and fighting are prohibited by law and equally unknown. Men do the coarser and heavier work, and women the finer and lighter. The following stanza from the excellent work of that most worthy, learned native Christian gentleman, Agi, known to history as Right Rev. Samuel Crowther, D. D., Bishop of Niger, fully illustrates the relative position of the sexes among the laboring classes to each other:

When the day dawns,
The trader takes his money,
The spinner takes *her* spindle,
The warrior takes his shield,

The weaver takes his batten,
The farmer wakes himself and his hoe,
The hunter wakes with his fiddle and his bow.

Here, of six vocations named in the stanza, there is but one, the *spinner* assigned to woman, the identical calling in which none but women among the most advanced of modern civilized nations are employed. We have italicized the word "her" in the third line of the stanza before "spindle," to arrest the attention of the reader. There is not even here any vocation assigned to women at all in the field, as is customary in civilized countries among Christian nations.

Such then are the people the polity of whose prospective civilization we have symbolized in these pages, together with that of their progenitors.

CHAPTER XVIII.

COMPARATIVE ELEMENTS OF CIVILIZATION.

It has been shown in a chapter on color that the white and black the pure European and pure African races, the most distinct and unlike each other in general external physical characteristics, are of equal vitality and equally enduring; absorbing and reproducing themselves as races, with all of their native external physical properties of complexion and hair.

That it may be indelibly fixed on every mind, we place on record the fact, that the races as such, especially white and black, are indestructible; that *miscegenation* as popularly understood—the running out of two races, or several, into a *new race*—cannot take place. A cross only produces one of a mixed race, and a continual cross from a half blood on either side will run into the pure original race, either white or black; the fourth cross on one side from the half-blood perfecting a whole blood. A general intermarriage of any two distinct races would eventually result simply in the destruction, the extinction of the less numerous of the two; that race which preponderates entirely absorbing the other.

The three original races in complexion and texture of hair are sterling; pure white, pure yellow, and pure black, with straight hair, and woolly hair; the two first being straight, and the other woolly. But it will be observed in the classes of mixed races, there is every variety of complexion and texture of hair. We have thus endeavored to be precise on a subject of such grave import to social science.

If indeed it were true, that what is implied by miscegenation could take place—the destruction of all or any of the three original rules by the formation of a new race to take the place of either or all—then, indeed, would the works of God be set at naught, his designs and purposes thwarted, and his wisdom confounded by the crafty schemes of poor, mortal, feeble man. Nay, verily, as long as earth endures, so long shall the original races in their purity, as designed by God, the Creator of all things, continue the three sterling races—yellow, black and white—naming them in the order given in Genesis of Shem, Ham and Japheth.

The sterling races, when crossed, can reproduce themselves into their original purity, as before stated. The offspring of any two of the sterling races becomes a mixed race. That mixed race is an abnormal race. Either of the two sterling races which produced the abnormal race may become the resolvent race. That is, when the offspring of a mixed or abnormal race marries to a person of sterling race, black or white, their offspring is a quadroon ; and if that quadroon intermarries on the same side, and the intermarriage so continue to the fourth cross on the same side, the offspring of this fourth intermarriage, is an octaroon (whether black or white), and therefore becomes a pure blood.   The race continuing the cross to its purity is the resolvent race, and each offspring of the cross till the fourth, is an abnormal race, when the fourth becomes sterling or pure blooded.   Hence, to speak of a mixed race as being changed by a resolvent process, simply means that the change is being made by one race alone, which must result in normal purity of either black or white, as the case may be.

The Malays, as stated in another part of this work, we regard not as an original or pure, but a mixed or abnormal race, possessing every feature, the complexion and texture of hair, known to the three original races, with many of these characteristics not belonging to either.   The Malays, no doubt, are an abnormal race, composed of the three original races, formed by an intermingling of the followers of the various invaders of Egypto-Ethiopian, Persian, Assyrian, Parthian, Greeko-Macedonian and Tartar conquerors, who have made conquests from time to time with the original natives of the Malay countries.

The natives of Australia, Van Dieman's Land, New Zealand, Borneo, Papua or New Guinea, are fair specimens of this race of people, who in time, no doubt, will become extinct by the European race fast settling among them, and the Mongolian, who will become resolvent races.   It is observable that these Malays, in their characteristics of features, complexion and hair,

differ more from each other than any other people as a race.
They vary from "snowy white to sooty," showing thereby that
they are not a fixed race, but a mixed, an abnormal race, which
has frequently been interrupted by different preponderating, and
thereby for the time, resolvent races.   In this we have a fair
evidence in the natives of Papua, or New Guinea.   And who
can doubt the fact, that the African once preponderated and
was the resolvent race among them?   These Malays, though they
might preponderate, never could become a resolvent race to
either of the sterling or original races.   Because, being themselves a mixed race, they could only produce a mixture, though
they intermarried to the fourth cross, such an offspring would
not be a pure blood.   To absorb and reproduce, the race must
be sterling; hence, it is resolvent.   There is no doubt but that
the time will come when there will be but the three original
sterling races as grand divisions of people on the face of the
whole earth, with their natural complexions of yellow, black and
white.

Finally, the African race in Africa should not be adjudged
by those portions of that race found out of Africa.   The difference is too great for comparison.   Untrammeled in its native
purity, the race is a noble one, and worthy to emulate the noble
Caucasian and Anglo-Saxon, now at the top round of the ladder
of moral and intellectual grandeur in the progress of civilization.

The regeneration of the African race can only be effected
by its own efforts, the efforts of its own self, whatever aid may
come from other sources; and it must in this venture succeed,
as God leads the movement and his hand guides the way.   And
now the advanced civilization of the Christianity of the world is
called upon to recognize an overture to their consideration.

"Princes shall come out of Egypt; Ethiopia shall soon stretch forth her hands unto God." Ps. lxviii. 31.

With faith in this blessed promise, thank God, in this our grand advent into Africa, we want

No kettle-drums nor flageolets,
Bag-pipes, trombones nor bayonets,

but with an abiding trust in God our Heavenly King, we shall boldly advance, singing the sweet songs of redemption, in the regeneration of our race and restoration of our father-land from the gloom and darkness of superstition and ignorance, to the glorious light of a more than pristine brightness—the light of the highest godly civilization.